"I was once in a ___ ___ ___ ___ _in Bed._"

"Did you have a big role?"

"No, just toast and marmalade."

• • •

"Why is it dangerous to play cards in the jungle?"

"'Cause there are too many cheetahs about."

• • •

"Come on, Daphne, do your homework."

"Oh, Dad...!"

"Do it now, please. Homework never killed anyone so far as I know."

"So why should I be the first?"

• • •

"What's the difference between an Indian elephant and an African elephant?"

"About three thousand miles."

1,000 MORE JOKES FOR KIDS

Michael Kilgarriff

BALLANTINE BOOKS • NEW YORK

Copyright © 1982 by Michael Kilgarriff

All rights reserved under International and Pan-American Copyright Conventions. Published in the United States by Ballantine Books, a division of Random House, Inc., New York, and simultaneously in Canada by Random House of Canada Limited, Toronto.

ISBN 0-345-34034-5

This edition published by arrangement with Ward Lock Ltd.

Printed in Canada

First Ballantine Books Edition: March 1987

23 22 21 20 19

Acknowledgments

I would like to express my gratitude to the following for so kindly permitting me to invade their classrooms and meetings in quest of the material for this book: the Headmistress, Miss M. J. Percy, of Notting Hill and Ealing High School (G.P.D.S.T.) and to Miss Ross and the pupils of Skipton House; the Headmistress, Mrs. James, the staff and pupils of Beacon House School, London, W.5; the Headmaster, Mr. V. S. McQueen, the staff and pupils of Montpelier Middle School, London W.5; Brown Owl (Mrs. O'Shaughnessy) and the girls of the 20th Ealing (St. Benedict's) Brownie Pack; Akela (Mr. Ken Frith) and the boys of the 9th Ealing Cub Pack; the Captain (Miss Julia Shipton) and the girls of the 20th Ealing (St. Benedict's) Guide Troop. And my thanks are also due to my father, Joseph C. Kilgarriff, for his valuable assistance.

Michael Kilgarriff

Contents

Letter to the author from his dear old mom

Dear Son,

Your Dad and I are so pleased to hear you are writing another book of jokes. We think it is ever so clever of you—but then you always were the bright one of the family. I remember you coming top of the class when you were fourteen. Your Dad and I were so proud, even if the other kids were only eight. And then came the great day when you went to Harvard University—what a pity it was shut...

I'm writing this letter slowly, by the way, because I know you can't read fast.

You won't know the old house when you next visit us— we have moved. It is very nice here but the washing machine doesn't seem to be working properly. In fact I've only used it once: I put in six shirts, pushed the handle, and I haven't seen them since.

Dad has a wonderful new job, with about five hundred people under him. He cuts the grass at the cemetery. Your sister Mary had a baby this morning but I haven't found out whether it is a boy or a girl so I don't know yet if you

1

are an aunt or an uncle. Your Uncle Patrick drowned last week in a vat of whiskey at the distillery in Dublin where he was working. Some of his pals tried to save him but he fought them off bravely.

It only rained twice this week—first for three days and then for four days. Monday was so windy one of the chickens laid the same egg four times.

I must write quicker now because my pen's running out.

We had a nasty letter from Mr. Coffin the undertaker. He said that if the bill for your Granny's funeral wasn't paid in seven days—up she comes.

I have had all my teeth taken out and a new fireplace put in.

Your loving,

P.S. I was going to send you $10.00 but I had already sealed the envelope.

Acting Stupid

"Did you see that outdoor show in the park last week?"

"Yes, I did. Terrible! It was so bad that half an hour after it started four trees got up and walked out!"

"I've been in films, you know," boasted the small-time actor to the wide-eyed young girl.

"Have you really?" she breathed admiringly.

"Oh yes. Did you see *Star Wars*?"

"Yes, I did indeed."

"So did I—excellent film, wasn't it . . . ?"

"Did you see *Lassie Come Home*?"

"Yes."

"I played the lead."

"What other films have you been in?"

"Unfortunately my best film wasn't released."

"Oh, why not?"

"It escaped."

3

"So you do bird impressions, eh?" said the theatrical agent.

"That's right, sir."

"What kind of bird impressions?"

"I eat worms."

"I finished a film last week."

"Did you?"

"Yes, I should have it back from the drug store tomorrow."

"I was once in a play called *Breakfast In Bed*."

"Did you have a big role?"

"No, just toast and jam."

"Oh dear," said the singer as he was about to go on stage, "I've got a frog in my throat."

"Then I should let the frog sing," said a rival vocalist, "It's got a better voice than you!"

"I was on TV last night."

"Were you?"

"Yes. When I'm drunk I'll sleep anywhere."

The effect of TV commercials on young viewers can be gauged from this version of part of the Lord's Prayer, as rendered by a small boy: "Give us this day our oven-fresh, slow-baked, vitamin-enriched, protein-packed, nourishing, delicious, wholemeal daily bread!"

"What sort of an act do you do?"

"I bend over backwards and pick up a handkerchief with my teeth."

"Anything else?"

"Then I bend over backwards and pick up my teeth."

"What sort of an act do you do?"

"I catch razor-sharp butcher's cleavers in my teeth!"

"In your teeth?!"

"Sure—I suppose you think I'm smiling..."

A circus proprietor caught his animal trainer thrashing one of the eleven performing elephants mercilessly. "Stop that!" he yelled, "What do you think you're doing, beating a valuable animal like that?"

"Coming out of the ring this afternoon he slipped, sir," said the trainer.

"That's no reason to punish him so severely."

"Oh, no? When he slipped he pulled the tails out of your other ten elephants!"

"Why did John Travolta break his leg?"

"Why?"

"'Cause he slipped on *Grease*."

One keen John Travolta fan went to the barber's and asked for a John Travolta hairstyle. The barber sat him down and began to wield the scissors enthusiastically—rather too enthusiastically, thought the customer.

"Are you sure you know what I mean by a John Travolta hairstyle?" he asked.

"Certainly, sir, don't you worry," said the barber confidently, snipping away. The customer became increasingly worried as his hair became shorter and shorter; when the barber then took up an electric razor and, in one swift movement, shaved a bald patch right across his head from ear to ear, he became positively frantic.

"What are you doing?" he yelled "I thought you said you knew what a John Travolta hairstyle was?"

"And so I do," said the indignant barber, "I saw him in *The King and I* fourteen times!"

The conceited comedian sought out the stage manager, saying petulantly, "I've just seen the running order of the show. You can't put an artiste of my reputation on after the performing monkeys!"

"Yes, you're right," mused the stage manager, "your acts are rather similar..."

"I used to be in show business. I had a very spectacular act."

"What did you do?"

"I used to dive into a wet sponge from a height of fifty feet. But then I broke my neck."

"Did you miss the sponge?"

"No. Some idiot squeezed it dry."

"I had a nasty shock while I was doing my act last night," said the comedian to a pal.

"What happened?"

"There was this guy in the front row—I thought he was laughing from ear to ear, but then just as I was finishing I saw he'd cut his throat!"

Did you hear about the actor who was so keen to get the part of Long John Silver that he had his leg cut off? He still didn't get the job—it was the wrong one.

Did you hear about the teenage boy who ran away with a circus? The police made him bring it back.

"I'm desperate to get a job as an actress."
  "Why don't you break your leg?"
  "Break my leg?"
  "Sure—then you'd be in a cast for months!"

Pets' Corner
or animal crackers

"My dog's got no legs. I call him Cigarette."

"Why?"

"'Cause every night I take him out for a drag."

"I did have a shock yesterday with my Binkie."

"You mean your parakeet?"

"Yes, poor little thing. I'd filled my lighter just before letting him out of his cage for his exercise, and I hadn't noticed that I'd spilled some of the fuel on the sideboard. Well, Binkie spotted it and before I could stop him he'd flown on to the sideboard and taken two or three beakfuls!"

"What happened?"

"Well, he gave a strangled squawk, flew straight up and hit the ceiling, and then flew three times around the room, going faster and faster!"

"Ooooh!"

"Then he flew out into the hall, into the kitchen, out of the kitchen back into the hall, up the stairs and into the bathroom. He flew straight at the mirror, smacked his little head—crack—against the glass and then fell into the sink. And there he lay, prone, not moving!"

"Was he dead?"

"No, he'd just run out of gas."

Last time Horace went to the zoo he got into trouble for feeding the monkeys . . . he fed them to the lions.

Two flies were on a cornflakes box. "Why are we running so fast?" asked one.

"Because," said the second, "it says 'tear along dotted line!'"

"Do you serve teetotalers?" asked the man in the bar.

"Of course we do, sir," replied the bartender.

"Right. A beer for me and two teetotalers for my crocodile here."

"I see you've got a new dog. Is he a watchdog?"

"Yes, he watches television."

"Have you had him long?"

"Only two weeks and already he's a one-man dog. He only bites me."

"I used to think I was a dog, but the doctor cured me."

"So you're all right now."

"Yes, I'm fine. Here—feel my nose."

"My parakeet lays square eggs."

"That's amazing! Can it talk as well?"

"Yes, but only one word."

"What's that?"

"Ouch!"

"Daddy, there's a man at the door with a bill."

"It must be a duck with a hat on."

The swing doors of the Wild West saloon crashed open and in came Little Pete, red with fury. "All right!" he raged, "all right! Who did it? What goldarned varmint painted my horse blue?"

And the huge figure of Black Joke, notorious gunfighter and town thug rose from a chair by the door.

"It was me, shrimp," he drawled, bunching his gigantic fists, "what about it?"

"Oh, well, er," stammered Little Pete wretchedly, "all I wanted to say was ... er ... when are you going to give it another coat?"

A man in a bar with his Labrador at his feet was intrigued to see another dog owner enter the bar. "That's a strange-looking dog you have there," he said.

"Yes, he is rather," said the newcomer, "but he's a great fighter."

"Is he now?" said the Labrador owner, "I bet he isn't as good a fighter as my Fang here."

"All right—how much do you bet?"

"Ten dollars."

"You're on."

So the two men took their dogs out into the bar parking lot where a tremendous fight ensued. Eventually the Labrador crawled, battered and bloody, his tail between his legs, to his master's side.

"That's ten dollars you owe me," said the owner of the strange-looking dog.

"I never thought I'd see Fang defeated," said the loser's master, handing over the money, "especially by such an odd-looking dog as yours."

"Yes, he does look a little peculiar," agreed the winner's master, "but he looked even odder before I shaved his mane off."

What is the difference between unlawful and illegal? Unlawful means against the law and illegal is a sick bird.

The huge lion was stalking proudly through the jungle when he came upon a leopard. "Leopard!" snarled the lion menacingly, "who is the King of the Jungle?"

"You are, Lion!" said the leopard nervously, and slunk away. Further down the jungle path the lion met a monkey. "Raaaarrrrgh!" roared the lion. "Monkey! Who is the King of the Jungle?"

"Oh, you are, Lion," said the monkey, cowering away, "no question about it!"

Further still down the jungle path the lion confronted an elephant. With his tail lashing, his magnificent mane bristling, his teeth bared and his claws fully exposed, the lion glared aggressively at the gray lumbering beast.

"Elephant!" commanded the lion, "who is the King of the Jungle?"

And without a word the elephant picked up the lion in his trunk and hurled him smack against a tree; he then picked up the dazed lion again and slammed him down on the ground—two, three, four times—and finally threw the by-now-semiconscious lion into a thick bramble patch.

"All right, all right!" mumbled the bleeding, battered, crumpled lion, "no need to get cross just because you don't know the answer!"

Why are parrots always clever? Because they suck seed (succeed).

"Peter! Stop pulling the dog's tail like that!"

"But it's him that's doing the pulling, Mom!"

Why is it dangerous to play cards in the jungle? 'Cause there are too many cheetahs about.

"My new horse is very well-mannered."
   "That's nice."
   "Yes, isn't it? Every time we come to a jump he stops and lets me go first!"

A large sailing ship was at anchor off the coast of Mauritius, and two dodos watched the sailors rowing ashore. "We'd better hide," said the first dodo.
   "Why?" asked the second.
   "Because," said the first, "we're supposed to be extinct, silly!"

Name nine animals from Africa. Eight elephants and a giraffe.

Name four animals of the cat family. Mommy cat, Daddy cat, and their two kittens.

When is a man-eating tiger likely to enter a house? When the door is open.

A policeman strolling on his beat one day was astonished to see a man walking towards him with a fully grown African lion on a leash.

"Hey!" said the policeman, "you can't walk around with a lion like that. Take him to the Zoo."

"Oh, all right, officer," said the lion owner, and away he went.

But the next day the policeman was again confronted with the man and his full-grown African lion walking along the pavement.

"Hey you!" yelled the policeman, "I thought I told you yesterday to take that lion to the Zoo?"

"I did," came the reply, "and today I'm taking him to the movies."

HER LADYSHIP: "Charters, there is a mouse in the west drawingroom."
BUTLER: "Very good, my lady. I'll ascertain whether the cat is at home."

"I had a laugh last Saturday," said the farmhand to his friends in the village bar.

"Why, what did you do?" they asked.

"I emptied a bottle o' Scotch in the cows' drinkin' water!"

"Did you, now? What happened to 'em?"

"They was all right—lapped it up! But next day didn't they have a hangunder!"

15

"I tried washing my parrot in Tide."

"Any good?"

"No, it died. It wasn't the Tide that killed him, though."

"What was it, then?"

"The spin dryer."

"Why are you crying, little boy?"

"I was thirsty—sob! sob!—and I swapped my dog for a bottle of lemonade! Boo-hoo!"

"And now you wish you had him back, eh?"

"Yeeesss! Waaaa!"

"Because you realize now how much you love him?"

"No—sob!—'cause I'm thirsty again!"

"My dog's bone idle."

"Is he?"

"Yesterday I was watering the garden, and he wouldn't lift a leg to help me!"

Why do prairie dogs howl all night long? 'Cause there aren't any trees on the prairie . . . just cactus.

Did you hear about the baby mouse who saw a bat? He ran home and told his mother he'd seen an angel . . .

The psychiatrist was surprised to see a tortoise come into his office.

"What can I do for you, Mr. Tortoise?" asked the psychiatrist.

"I'm terribly shy, doctor," said the tortoise, "I want you to cure me of that."

"No problem. I'll soon have you out of your shell."

"I love watching tennis," said the cat to his friend.

"Why?"

"I've got two brothers in that racket."

Why was the young kangaroo thrown out by his mother? For smoking in bed.

What did one germ say to the other germ? "Keep away— I've got a dose of penicillin."

Two sheep, walking in opposite directions, met in a country lane.

"Baaa," said the first sheep.

"Hee-haw!" said the second.

"Baaa!" said the first again, in a surprised tone.

"Hee-haw!" repeated the second.

"What are you up to?" asked the first sheep. "Sheep don't go 'hee-haw.'"

"But I'm a stranger around here," said the second.

"Doctor, doctor!" said the panic-stricken woman, "my husband was asleep with his mouth open, and he's swallowed a mouse! What shall I do?"

"Quite simple," said the doctor calmly. "You just tie a lump of cheese to a piece of string and lower it into your husband's mouth. As soon as the mouse takes a bite—haul it out."

"Oh, I see. Thank you, doctor. I'll go around to the fishmonger straight away and get a cod's head."

"What do you want a cod's head for?"

"Oh—I forgot to tell you. I've got to get the cat out first!"

Who would win a fight between an African lion and an African tiger? Neither—there aren't any tigers in Africa.

"Look at that speed!" said one hawk to another as the jet fighter plane hurtled over their heads.

"Hmph!" snorted the other. "You would fly fast too if your tail was on fire!"

"Look over there!" said the frightened skunk to his pal, "There's a human with a gun, and he's getting closer and closer! What are we going to do?"

To which the second skunk calmly replied, "Let us spray..."

A very intelligent boy was fortunate enough to be receiving a far better education than his parents had enjoyed, and his vocabulary far outstripped theirs. One day he came home from school and said, "Mommy, may I relate to you a narrative?"

"What's a narrative, Gerald?" she asked.

"A narrative, Mommy, is a tale."

"Oh, I see," said his mother nodding, and Gerald told her his story. At bedtime as he was about to go upstairs he said, "Shall I extinguish the light, Mommy?"

"What's extinguish?" she asked.

"Extinguish means to put out, Mommy," said brainy Gerald.

"Oh, I see. Yes, certainly."

The next day the parson came to tea and the family dog began to make a nuisance of himself, as dogs will, by begging for goodies from the table. "Gerald," said his mother, trying to impress, "take that dog by the narrative and extinguish him!"

A woman owned a parrot that could say only one thing— "Who is it?" For years and years she had been trying to teach it to extend its vocabulary, but it resolutely refused to utter anything other than "Who is it?"

One day she had sent for the plumber, and as she had to go out shopping she arranged for him to find the key under the mat outside the front door. The plumber duly arrived, found the key, let himself in and set to work. Naturally the parrot, hearing someone in the house with an unfamiliar tread, decided to give a recital. "Who is it?" called the parrot. "The plumber!" called the workman. Hearing a strange voice the parrot again decided to utter his one and only phrase. "Who is it?"

"The plumber!" came the response.

The parrot was not satisfied—he wanted to see who the stranger was. "Who is it?" he called again, and again the plumber yelled out "It's the plumber!" Again and again the bird called out "Who is it?" and again and again the poor bewildered plumber responded—"It's the plumber! *It's the Plumber!* IT'S THE PLUMBER!" Eventually in a fury he roamed the house, going from room to room, trying to find out who was calling him—but he failed to realize that it was the parrot. For a whole hour this went on, with him dashing around the house, growing increasingly desperate, and shouting out "It's the plumber!" until eventually the wretched man fainted clean away in the hall!

Just at that moment the mistress of the house entered, saw the unconscious figure on the carpet and said, "Oh! Who is it?"

The parrot replied, "It's the plumber!"

Two little skunks called In and Out were playing in the woods. Out went home, and his mother said, "Where's In?

Go and get him, there's a good boy." So Out went back into the woods and returned very shortly with his brother.

"That's a good boy," said Mother Skunk, "how did you find him so quickly?"

"Easy," said the little skunk, "In stinked..."

Two fleas were walking out of a cinema when they discovered it was raining hard.

"Shall we walk?" said one flea.

"No," said the other, "let's take a dog."

A man driving up the interstate one dark night was amazed to see a weird creature overtake him at tremendous speed. He accelerated in an attempt to catch up with it, but the creature was far too quick for him and dimly he saw it run off the highway at an exit. The driver, determined to try and find out what this extraordinary thing was, also turned off at the exit—just in time to see it jump over a hedge and disappear into some woods. Nearby stood a farmhouse; the driver stopped his car, walked up to the door and knocked.

"I'm sorry to bother you," said the driver to the farmer as he opened the door, "but I've just seen an extraordinary creature jump over your hedge and go into the woods. It was quite small and I think it had feathers, but it could run at fantastic speed. Have you any idea what it could be?"

21

"Oh yes," said the farmer, "that's one of my three-legged chickens. I've been breeding them specially."

"Three-legged chickens!" said the driver. "Why should you want to breed chickens with three legs?"

"So that when we have roast chicken for dinner," said the farmer, "my wife, my son and myself can have a leg each."

"Oh, I see," said the driver, nodding. "What do they taste like?"

"Don't know," said the farmer, "I haven't been able to catch one yet!"

How do you stop a skunk smelling? Put a clothespin on his nose!

"Mommy," said the baby polar bear, "am I one hundred percent pure polar bear?"

"Of course you are, son," said his Daddy, "Why do you ask?"

"'Cause I'm f-f-f-freezing!"

"Are we poisonous?" the baby snake asked his Mommy.

"Yes, dear," she replied. "Why do you ask?"

"'Cause I've just bitten my tongue!"

A rabbit walked into a bar and ordered ham on toast and a beer. After drinking his beer and eating his ham on toast he still felt hungry, so he ordered cheese on toast and another beer. After drinking his beer and eating his cheese on toast he *still* felt hungry, so he ordered sardines on toast and another beer. And just as he was finishing his beer and his sardines on toast, he dropped down dead! The bartender, at a loss to know what to do with a dead rabbit customer, decided to bury him in the back garden; that night the ghost of the rabbit appeared to him. "Why did you die?" asked the frightened bartender, to which the rabbit replied, "Mixin' my toasts..." (Myxomatosis)

A little fledgling fell out of its nest and went crashing through the branches of the elm tree towards the ground.

"Are you all right?" called out an owl as the chick went hurtling past his perch.

"So far!" said the little bird.

Class Laughs

or are you trying to be funny, boy?

Young Timmy was on the carpet in the Principal's office. "I'm getting rather tired of seeing you here," said the Principal. "What is it this time?"

"Nothing, sir," said the indignant young scholar, "I was only doing what Mr. Jackson told me."

"Really?" said the Principal with a sigh. "Are you sure you weren't being insolent again?"

"No, sir. Mr. Jackson got all upset with me over my homework and said, 'What do you think I am?' So I told him!"

Norman left school with regret. He was sorry he'd ever had to go.

"You really must pay attention, Jenny," complained the long-suffering teacher. "After all—what are you in school for?"

"Er—to learn, ma'am?"

"Yes. Anything else?"

"Er—to play sports?"

"Yes. And why else are you here?"

"Er—because they came and got me, ma'am."

"Johnny, I've had a letter from your Principal. It seems you're very careless with your appearance."

"Am I, Dad?"

"Yes. You haven't appeared in school since last semester!"

"Now my motto in life," said the school chaplain, "is work hard, play hard and pray hard. How about you, Harriet?"

"My motto is let bygones be bygones."

"That's good. Why did you choose that?"

"Then I wouldn't have to take any history classes!"

The three friends were walking home from school. "What shall we do this afternoon?" said one. "I know," said the second, let's spin a coin. If it comes down heads let's go skating, and if it comes down tails let's go swimming."

"And if it comes down on its edge," said the third, "let's stay in and do our homework!"

Have you noticed, kids, how if you pass your exams everyone says you get your brains from your parents, but if you fail your exams everyone says you're stupid . . . ?

"How did you get on with your home ec exam, Sharon?"

"Well, Mom, I got eight out of ten for defrosting."

"Who was the first woman in the world, Becky?" asked the Religion teacher.

"Er—er—" floundered the little girl.

"I'll give you a clue. It's got something to do with an apple."

"Oh—Granny Smith, ma'am."

"What did your mother do yesterday morning, Vicky?"

"She done her shopping, ma'am."

"*Done* her shopping, Vicky? Where's your grammar?"

"She done her shopping as well, ma'am."

"Why aren't you writing, George?"

"I ain't got no pencil, sir."

"You ain't got no pencil? You have no pencil, you mean."

"Sir?"

"I have no pencil, he has no pencil, she has no pencil, we have no pencils."

"Gosh—who's stolen all the pencils!?"

"Give me a sentence starting with I, Mandy."

"Yes, ma'am. I is—"

"No, no, no, Mandy. You don't say 'I is,' you say 'I am.'"

"All right, ma'am. I am the ninth letter of the alphabet."

Barry was told by his teacher to bring three words or phrases to school the next day for discussion. Unable to think of anything suitable, Barry asked his big brother for a suggestion, but his big brother was listening intently to a new record he had just bought. "Shut up!" he roared, so Barry tried his big sister. "Sis," he asked plaintively, "I need three words or phrases for—" but his big sister was listening to the news on the radio and was quite uninterested in poor Barry's problems. "Be quiet!" she snapped, and so the boy tried his small brother, who was watching television. "Do you think you could—?" but Barry's small brother was furious at being interrupted while watching his favorite program. "It's Batman!" he shouted.

In class the next day, Barry's teacher addressed him. "Well, Barry," he said, "what words or phrases have you thought of?"

"Shut up," said Barry.

"How dare you, Barry!" cried the indignant teacher. "Do you want me to call the Principal?"

"Be quiet," said Barry, to the amazement of class and teacher alike.

"Don't talk to me like that!" roared the teacher. "Just who do you think I am?"

Poor Barry could only reply, "Batman!"

The teacher was warning the class about the dangers of going out in cold weather insufficiently clad. "There was once a boy," he said, "who was so eager to go out and play with his sled that he didn't put a coat or scarf on; he caught a chill, the chill led to pneumonia and he died!"

The teacher paused to allow the moral of this story to

sink in, when a small voice said, "What happened to the sled . . . ?"

"What would you like to be when you grow up, Tommy?"

"I'd like to be a teacher, sir."

"Would you, indeed? And why would you like to be a teacher?"

"'Cause I wouldn't have to do any more learning—I'd know everything by then!"

"Tracey, can you count up to ten?"

"Yes, ma'am. (*Counting on her fingers held at waist level*) "One, two, three, four, five, six, seven, eight, nine, ten."

"Very good, Tracey. Can you count any higher?"

"Yes," (*Counting again on her fingers from one to ten but this time with her hands above her head!*)

"Helen, if I had $1,000 in my right hand and $2,000 in my left hand, what would I have?"

"Riches, ma'am."

"Alfred, if I had 20 marbles in my right pants pocket, 20 marbles in my left pants pocket, 40 marbles in my right hip pocket and 40 marbles in my left hip pocket—what would I have?"

"Heavy pants, sir!"

"Simon, if I had eight apples in my right hand and ten apples in my left hand, what would I have?"

"Huge hands, sir."

"Julian, why are you late?"

"Sorry, sir. I overslept, sir."

"You mean you sleep at home as well?!"

"Christopher, give me a sentence with the word 'fascinate' in it."

"Yes, sir. Er—if I have a shirt with ten buttons and two of them fall off, I can only fasten eight!"

"Christina, give me a sentence containing the word 'centimeter'!"

"Yes, ma'am. Last summer, when my Granny was coming to stay with us, I was sent-to-meet-her."

"Harold," asked the math teacher, "which would you prefer: eight ice-cream cones or eighty ice-cream cones?"

"Eight, sir," replied Harold.

"Eight?" sneered the teacher, "don't you know the difference between eight and eighty?"

"Yes, sir," replied Harold calmly, "but I don't like ice cream."

"What is the most popular answer to schoolteachers' question?"

"I don't know."

"Correct."

"Come along, Daphne, do your homework."

"Oh, Dad . !"

"Do it now, please. Homework never killed anyone as far as I know."

"So why should I be the first?"

Why did the teacher have to wear sunglasses? Because his pupils were so bright

"Does your teacher like you?"

"I think so. She keeps putting kisses on my homework."

"Kenneth, name ten things with milk in them."

"Yes, sir. Milkshake, tea, coffee, cocoa, and—er— six cows."

Ian, who was known for his insolence, was taken by the scruff of his neck by the gym teacher to the Principal's office.

"What is it this time?" sighed the Principal.

"He called me a stupid, boring old jerk!" declared the angry gym teacher.

"Now, Principal, how would you like to be called a stupid, boring old jerk—supposing you weren't one?!"

"What's twelve times twelve?"

"One hundred and forty-four."

"Yes, that's good."

"Good? It's perfect!"

School meals are generally unpopular with those who have to eat them—and sometimes with good reason. "What kind of pie do you call this?" asked one schoolboy indignantly.

"What's it taste like?" asked the cook."

"Glue!"

"Then it's apple pie—the plum pie tastes like soap."

"Any complaints?" asked the teacher during school lunch.

"Yes, sir," said one bold boy, "these peas are awfully hard, sir."

The teacher dipped a spoon into the peas on the boy's plate and tasted them.

"They seem soft enough to me," he declared.

"Yes, they are *now*," agreed the boy, "I've been chewing them for the last half hour!"

"Any complaints?"

"Yes, sir. This."

"Tastes all right to me. That's excellent tea."

"But it isn't tea, sir. It's stew."

"And very good stew it is, too..."

"There's something I can do that nobody else in my school can do. Not even the teachers!"

"What's that?"

"Read my handwriting!"

"Do you obtain good SAT results?" asked the father of a prospective pupil.

"Oh, indeed we do," said the Principal of the expensive

private school. "We guarantee satisfaction—or we return the boy..."

"I think I'd like to join the Air Force," said the lad to the career adviser.

"You like flying, do you?"

"Yes, sir. As long as I can keep one foot on the ground."

"How are you doing in school?"

"I'm doing well in everything except classes."

"It's no good, sir," said the hopeless pupil to his English teacher, "I try to learn, but everything you say goes in both ears and out the other."

"Goes in both ears and out the other?" asked the puzzled teacher, "but you only have two ears, boy."

"You see, sir? I'm no good at math, either!"

"I thought I told you to stand at the end of the line!" said the teacher crossly at morning assembly.

"I did, sir," said the new boy miserably, "but there was someone there already!"

"You're looking well, young Hubert," said the visitor heartily.

"Yes, I am, aren't I?" agreed the boy. "Especially since I've just had angina, arteriosclerosis, tuberculosis, pneumonia, aphasia, hypertrophic cirrhosis, and eczema!"

"That's terrible!" exclaimed the visitor in concern, "to have had all those things at your tender age!"

"Yes," the lad agreed. "It was the hardest spelling test I've ever had!"

Brian Backtalk was living up to his reputation as the most argumentative boy in the school. Furious at being contradicted yet again, his teacher yelled at him. "That's enough from you! Who's the teacher here—you or me?"

"You, sir."

"Then why are you talking like an idiot?!"

"Sharon, name two pronouns."

"Who, me?"

"Correct."

BOY: "I'd like to follow the medical profession, sir."
CAREER ADVISER: "So you want to be a doctor?"
BOY: "No, an undertaker."

"Where are you from, Monckton?" the teacher asked the new boy in the class.

"Er—Dorset, sir," came the nervous reply.

"Dorset, eh? What part?"

"All of me, sir."

"How are you getting on with your exams?"

"Not bad. The questions are easy enough—it's the answers I have trouble with!"

"Can you count up to ten, Prunella?"

"Yes, ma'am. One, two, three, four, five, six, seven, eight, nine, ten."

"Very good. Now, can you go on from there?"

"Yes, ma'am. Jack, Queen, King!"

Matthew and Mark were twin boys who went to the same school, though in different classes. One night Matthew said to Mark, "I can't do my math homework! Can you help me?" Now Mark was very good at math and he finished off Matthew's homework in superfast time.

"I tell you what," said Mark, "why don't I take your place in your math class tomorrow?"

Matthew naturally agreed like a shot, and the substitution was successfully accomplished. Mark's brilliance astounded the math teacher, so much so that he began to get annoyed.

"Yes, excellent, I must say," he sneered. "You're so clever all of a sudden, aren't you? I suppose you even know what I'm thinking, eh?"

"Yes, sir," said the twin, "You're thinking that I'm Matthew but I'm not—I'm Mark!"

Why did Ken take his bike to school?
'Cause he wanted to drive his teacher up the wall!

Why did Ken take his ladder to school?
'Cause he wanted to go to High School!

Don't Make Me Cross!

WHAT DO YOU GET IF YOU CROSS...
- *a cat and an octagon?*
  An octopus.

- *a mink and a kangaroo?*
  A fur coat with very large pockets.

- *a bear and a skunk?*
  Winnie the Pyooh.

- *a giraffe and a hedgehog?*
  An eight-foot toothbrush.

- *a baby goat and a hedgehog?*
  A stuck-up kid.

- *a centipede and a parrot?*
  A walkie-talkie.

- a bee and a skunk?
  Something that stings and stinks at the same time.

- the white of an egg and a pound of gunpowder?
  A boom-meringue.

- a snowman and a man-eating shark?
  Frostbite.

- a cat and a lemòn?
  A sourpuss.

- a kangaroo and an elephant?
  Great big holes all over Australia.

- a shag rug and an elephant?
  A great big pile in your living room.

- a fish and two elephants?
  Swimming trunks.

The Same Only Different

WHAT'S THE DIFFERENCE BETWEEN...
- *a jeweler and a jailer?*
  One sells watches and the other watches cells.

- *a baker and a heavy sleeper?*
  One bakes the bread and the other breaks the bed.

- *a butcher and a light sleeper?*
  One weighs a steak and the other stays awake.

- *Hitler and a dog?*
  One goes like this (*raise arm*) and the other goes like this (*raise leg*).

- *a forged dollar bill and an insane rabbit?*
  One is bad money and the other is a mad bunny.

- *a storm cloud and a child being spanked?*
  One pours with rain and the other roars with pain!

- a tailor and a horse trainer?
One mends tears and the other tends mares.

- a railway guard and a teacher?
One minds the train and the other trains the mind.

- an Indian elephant and an African elephant?
About three thousand miles.

- elephants and fleas?
Elephants can have fleas but fleas can't have elephants.

- a hill and a pill?
One goes up and other goes down.

Doctor's Rounds

"Doctor, doctor! My family thinks I'm mad!"
  "Why is that?"
  "I like sausages."
  "There's nothing strange about that. I like sausages too."
  "Really? You must come and see my collection—I've got thousands!"

"Doctor, doctor! I've only got fifty-nine seconds to live."
  "Wait a minute, please..."

"Doctor, doctor! Everyone keeps ignoring me."
  "Next, please."

"Doctor, doctor! I feel like a pack of cards."
  "All right, I'll deal with you later."

"Doctor, doctor! I keep thinking I'm a curtain."
  "Pull yourself together."

"Doctor, doctor! I feel like a goat."
  "How long have you been like this?"
  "Since I was a kid."

"Doctor, doctor! I keep thinking I'm a bridge!"
  "Well, well, well—what's come over you today?"

"Doctor, doctor! I think I've got measles!"
  "That's a rash thing to say."

"Doctor, doctor! I've swallowed a spoon!"
  "Lie down and don't stir."

"Doctor, doctor! Can you give me something for my liver?"
  "How about a pound of onions?!"

"Doctor, doctor! What are you writing on my ankle?"
  "Just a footnote."

"Doctor, doctor! Can you give me something for my flat feet?"

"How about a bicycle pump?"

"Doctor, doctor! I feel like painting myself gold all over."

"You've got a gilt complex."

"Doctor, doctor! If I take these green pills will I get better?"

"Well, nobody I've given them to has ever come back."

"Doctor, doctor! I keep thinking I'm a fridge!"

"Shut your mouth—you're shining your light right in my eyes."

"Doctor, doctor! I feel like an apple!"

"Well, come over here—I won't bite you."

"Doctor, doctor! I keep thinking I'm invisible!"

"Who's that?"

"Doctor, doctor! I can't sleep!"

"Sleep on the edge of the bed. You'll soon drop off."

"Doctor, doctor! I keep thinking I'm a ten-dollar bill!"
    "Well, go shopping. You need the change."

"Doctor, doctor! I keep thinking I'm a doorknob!"
    "All right, all right! Don't fly off the handle..."

"Doctor, doctor! I feel like an old sweater!"
    "Well, I'll be darned!"

"Doctor, doctor! I feel like a bar of soap!"
    "That's life, boy..."

"Doctor, doctor! I feel like a window!"
    "Really? Where's the pain?"

"Doctor, doctor! I feel like a bell."
    "Take these pills and give me a ring."

"Doctor, doctor! I feel like a piano."
    "Wait while I make some notes."

"Doctor, doctor! I feel like a parrot."
  "Just perch there a moment."

"Doctor, doctor! I feel like a strawberry!"
  "You are in a jam, aren't you?"

"Doctor, doctor! I can't stop telling lies!"
  "I don't believe you."

"Doctor, doctor! I feel like a car!"
  "Just park yourself over there."

"Doctor, doctor! I feel like there are two of me!"
  "Very well, I'll see you one at a time."

"Doctor, doctor! I keep feeling like a pane of glass."
  "I thought as much—next time don't come in through
the window."

"Doctor, doctor! I feel like a pile of bricks."
  "You'll find them very hard to swallow."

"Doctor, doctor! I'm at death's door!"
  "Don't worry—I'll pull you through."

"Doctor, doctor! I want to lose 20 pounds of excess fat."
  "I'll amputate your head."

"Doctor, doctor! I'm having trouble breathing."
  "I'll soon put a stop to that."

"Doctor, doctor! Can you cure my acne?"
  "I'm making no rash promises."

"Doctor, doctor! I'm becoming invisible!"
  "Yes, I can see you're not all there."

"Doctor, doctor! You've taken out my adenoids, my tonsils,
my gall bladder, my varicose veins, and my appendix, but
I still don't feel well!"
  "That's quite enough out of you."

"Doctor, doctor! I feel like a sheep!"
  "That's baaaaaad!"

"Doctor, doctor! I feel like an apple!"
"We must get to the core of this."

"Doctor, doctor! I feel like an orange!"
"Have you tried playing squash!"

"Doctor, doctor! I feel like an electric wire!"
"How shocking!"

"Doctor, doctor! I feel like a dog!"
"Sit!"

"Doctor, doctor! I've just swallowed a pencil!"
"Sit down and write your name."

Heard of
Elephants...?

How does an elephant come down a tree?
It stands on a leaf and waits for autumn.

How does an elephant go up a tree?
It stands on an acorn and waits for it to grow.

Why do elephants paint their feet yellow?
So they can hide upside down in a bowl of custard...
you've never found an elephant in your custard, have you?
No? Works well, then, doesn't it?

What do elephants play in the back of a VW bug?
Squash.

Why did the elephant sit on the tomato?
    He wanted to play squash.

Why do elephants have trunks?
    They'd look silly with suitcases, wouldn't they?

If you see an elephant sitting on a chair—what time is it?
    Time to get a new chair.

"How big is an elephant?"
    "What kind of elephant?"
    "A big one."
    "How big?"

Everyone knows an elephant never forgets—but then what does he have to remember?

How do you get four elephants in a VW bug?
    Two in the back and two in the front.

How do you get a rhinoceros in a VW bug?
    Chuck one of the elephants out.

When do elephants have sixteen feet?
  When there are four of them.

Did you hear about the elephant who was always drunk?
  He kept seeing pink people.

Why can't you put an elephant in a sandwich?
  'Cause it's too heavy to lift.

How can you tell if an elephant's been in your bed?
  'Cause it'll be full of peanut shells.

How can you tell if an elephant's been in the fridge?
  'Cause there'll be giant footprints in the butter.

What do elephants have that no other animal has?
  Baby elephants.

How do you get down off an elephant?
  You can't—you get it off a swan.

Why can't an elephant ride a bike?
  'Cause he hasn't got a thumb to ring the bell.

What do you get if a herd of elephants tramples Batman and Robin?
  Flatman and Ribbon.

Who is Tarzan's favorite singer?
  Harry Elefante.

Why is an elephant large, gray, hairy, and wrinkled?
  'Cause if he was small, white, hairless, and smooth he'd be an aspirin.

How do you stop an elephant passing through the eye of a needle?
  Tie a knot in his tail.

How do you know when there's an elephant in your custard?
  When it's *ever* so lumpy.

Why did the elephant cross the road?
'Cause it was the chicken's day off.

How do you know when an elephant is hiding under your bed?
'Cause when you wake up your nose is squashed against the ceiling.

What do you do when an elephant sits on your hanky?
Wait for him to get up.

Tom, Dick, and Harry (and others)

Tom, Dick, and Harry were standing on the edge of the cliff. With them was an eccentric but wealthy lady who said, "To whichever of you is brave enough to jump over the cliff I will give one million dollars!" Despite the extreme danger, the lure of one million dollars was too much for Harry. "God save Ireland!" he cried, and jumped over the edge. But poor Harry came to a sticky end, just a few seconds later, on the rocks at the foot of the eighty-foot drop. Despite this tragedy the lure of one million dollars was similarly too tempting for Dick. "God save Scotland!" he cried—and jumped to his death also. Tom, mesmerized by the prospect of one million dollars but courteous to the end, raised his hat and gave a courtly bow, "After you, Madam," he said, gesturing to the edge . . .

Tom, Dick, and Harry were traveling in the desert. Arriving at a small village they could find nowhere to sleep but a strange inn whose landlord, though willing to take them in for the night, could offer only a bed of fire, a bed of nails, and a bed of fleas. In the morning, they compared notes over breakfast.

"That bed of fire was awful," said Tom. "Very uncomfortable. I didn't sleep a wink, and I'm scorched all over."

"I had a bad night, too," said Dick. "That bed of nails was dreadful. I'm covered with little holes."

"I slept fine," declared Harry. "My bed of fleas was no trouble at all. I just killed one flea and all the rest went to the funeral!"

Again we find Tom, Dick, and Harry on the edge of a cliff, and again they are accompanied by a lady. "I will throw this watch over the edge," she said, "and whoever can run down the steps and catch it before it hits the ground can marry me."

Now, this lady was young, pretty and very rich, so the three aspirants to her hand made ready for the run of their lives. The watch was thrown over and Tom hurtled down the steps; but he was little more than a quarter of the way down when the watch smashed to pieces on the rocks eighty feet below. The lady produced a second watch, and on her hurling that into space Dick also tried to beat it to the bottom. To no avail—he got no more than a quarter of the way down before the second watch was smashed to smithereens.

"My turn now," said Harry.

"We'll have to try tomorrow," said the lady, "for I've run out of watches."

"That's no problem," said Harry, "you can throw

mine." He removed it from his wrist, handed it to the pretty, young and wealthy lady, and sauntered to the top step. The watch soared over the edge of the cliff and Harry began a leisurely walk down, to the amazement of Tom and Dick—and of course, the lady herself.

Twenty minutes later Harry appeared again at the top of the cliff steps. He walked smiling over to the young lady and handed her the watch—intact!

"You caught it, then?" gasped the lady.

"Sure I caught it," replied Harry, "no trouble at all, at all."

"But how did you get down in time?" demanded Tom and Dick.

"It was easy," said Harry, "I always keep my watch half an hour slow."

Once more Tom, Dick, and Harry are traveling in the desert when their jeep breaks down some ten miles from the nearest village. There is nothing for it but to walk across the burning sand, under the cruel pitiless sun, if they are not to die of thirst. Tom takes an umbrella, Dick a water-bottle, and Harry rips off the door of the jeep and carries that with him. But they had only walked two or three miles when, quite unexpectedly, salvation appeared in the shape of a camel caravan. The leader of the caravan agreed to assist Tom, Dick, and Harry to the village; he gave them food and drink and a camel each to ride upon.

"But tell me," he said to Tom. "Why do you carry

this umbrella in the desert? There has not been rain in these parts for many years."

"It isn't to protect me from rain," replied Tom, "but to protect me from the sun."

"Ah!" said the leader of the caravan. "Truly this man is wise. And you, my friend," he said to Dick, "why do you carry this bottle?"

"I decided," answered Dick, "that thirst would be the greatest problem if we had to walk ten miles across the hot sand, so I emptied out the water and filled it with good Scotch whiskey!"

"Ah!" said the leader of the caravan. "Truly this man is wise. And you, my friend," he said to Harry, "why do you carry the door of your vehicle?"

"I was also worried about the heat," said Harry, "so I thought if I carried the door and it got too hot I could always roll down the window."

Tom, Dick, and Harry were invited to a Fancy Dress Ball. They arrived at the Ball with Tom wearing false ears and eyebrows. "What have you come as?" asked the host. "Mr. Spock," replied Tom. Dick was wearing black boots, black trousers and a red jumper. "And what have you come as?" asked the host. "Scotty," replied Dick. Harry was dressed as a tree. "And what have you come as?" asked the host. "The captain's log," replied Harry.

Tom, Dick, and Wong were taking part in a balloon race from London to Edinburgh. As they floated northward Tom looked down and sighed, "Ah, my beautiful England!" As they sailed over the border Dick looked down and sighed, "Ah, my beautiful Scotland!" So Wong threw a cup overboard and sighed, "Ah, my beautiful China!"

Tom, Dick, and Harry all had the misfortune to fall into the hands of a band of brigands. "You have no rich relatives who can pay me a large ransom for your release," said the brigand chief, "so you must be executed. But I am a merciful man, and I promise you your death will be quick. You will be executed by guillotine—I am assured it is quite painless; it is all over in a second."

So Tom was led to the guillotine; he knelt down, the lever was pulled—but the huge, heavy blade stuck fast! "It is the Hand of Providence!" declared the brigand chief. "Release him!" Then Dick was led to the guillotine —and again the blade refused to descend. It is the Hand of Providence!" declared the brigand chief. "Release him!" And Harry was then led to the guillotine. "I want none of that!" shouted Harry. "It isn't quick at all. Shoot me instead!"

Tom, Dick, and Harry had the misfortune to fall into the hands of another band of brigands. "You are miserable worms with no one to pay me a large ransom to save your verminous hides," said the brigand chief, "so you must be executed by guillotine—I am assured it is quite painless, and all will be over in a second."

So Tom was led to the guillotine; he knelt down, the lever was pulled and the huge, heavy blade began to drop. But just inches from his exposed neck the blade jammed! "It is the Hand of Providence!" declared the brigand chief. "Release him!" Then Dick was led to the guillotine—and again, inches from his exposed neck, the huge heavy blade jammed. "It is the Hand of Providence!" declared the brigand chief. "Release him!" And Harry was led to the guillotine; he knelt down—but just as the lever was about to be pulled he looked up and said, "Hold it a minute! There's a little bit of wood sticking out—that's the trouble with it . . ."

Tom, Dick, and Harry were stranded on a desert island. Wandering disconsolately around the small island looking for food and water, Tom accidently kicked a bottle lying in the grass; the bottle broke, releasing a genie! "O, Master!" said the genie, "for ten thousand years have I been imprisoned in that bottle. For you and your companions I can grant three wishes. But choose wisely, for I can grant three wishes and three wishes only."

"Do you mean three wishes between us, or three wishes each?" asked Tom.

"Three wishes between you, O Master," answered the genie. "You have one wish each. Choose with care."

"My wish is quite simple," said Tom, "I wish to be taken home."

"Your wish is my command!" said the genie. He waved his hands—and Tom vanished.

"Yes, I'd like the same," said Dick, "I wish to be taken home."

"Your wish is my command!" said the genie. He waved his hands—and Dick disappeared. "And your wish, O Master?" said the genie to Harry.

"I'm very lonely here without the other two," said Harry, "so I wish they were back here with me!"

So Tom, Dick, and Harry were still on their desert island with nothing to eat but grass. They were getting hungrier and hungrier, when one day Tom said, "Look! there's a meat pie floating in the sea!" So Dick, who was the best swimmer, plunged into the sea and returned triumphantly with the pie. "Oh, we can't eat that!" said Harry. "It's soaked with seawater; we'd better leave it in the sun to dry off."

"It's very small," said Tom. "It isn't worth dividing it between us, and in any case I think I should have it all to myself because I saw it first."

"And who swam out, risking the sharks and the coral, to bring it to shore?" said Dick. "If anyone should have it all to himself, it is I."

"Now wait a minute, boys," said Harry. "If anyone had eaten it without drying out the salt water he'd have made himself very ill indeed, so I think I should have it all to myself."

After much arguing they decided to leave the pie overnight; the person who had the best dream would have the privilege of eating the entire pie for breakfast. In the morning Tom said, "I dreamed I was back in my beautiful hometown. Now, you can't have a finer dream than that!"

Harry said, "I dreamed I was back in my dear wife's arms—and no man can have a finer dream than that!"

And Dick said, "Well, chaps, I dreamed that I was starving—so I woke up and ate the pie!"

Tom, Dick, and Harry were caught in a storm in the country. They spied a big old house just off the road, to which they ran for shelter. But to their calls and knocks came no answer; the house seemed deserted. And rather spooky as well . . suddenly the door swung open of its own accord, the hinges squeaking eerily. But still no one was to be seen. Plucking up his courage, Tom crept into the hallway, and there, on a small table, lay a five dollar bill! But as he reached out a greedy hand to take the money, a sepulchral voice rang out:

"I'm the ghost of Abel Mabel,
That five dollar bill must stay on the table!"

With a shriek of terror Tom dashed out of the house, past his two companions and into the storm. Dick looked at Harry, shrugged, and crept cautiously into the hallway. He also saw the five dollar bill and stretched out a hand to steal it. And again that awful, disembodied voice rang out:

"I'm the ghost of Abel Mabel,
That five dollar bill must stay on the table!"

Dick, his nerve shattered, dashed out of the house,

yelling with fright, and into the storm. Harry looked after him, squared his shoulders, and marched into the hallway. There lay the five dollar bill, and Harry also could not resist the temptation. As his hand stretched towards the bill, the strange voice rang out for a third time:

"I'm the ghost of Abel Mabel,
That five dollar bill must stay on the table!"
To which Harry replied
"I'm the grandson of Davy Crockett—
That five dollar bill belongs in my pocket!"

Caught in another storm, Tom, Dick, and Harry attempted to take shelter in another sinister-looking house. It was night, no lights showed in the windows, and the whole atmosphere was distinctly uneasy. Again, nobody answered to the trio's repeated shouts and knocks, and again the door creaked open of its own accord. In went Harry, feeling his way along the hall, scarcely daring to breathe; when on reaching the foot of the stairs he heard a weird, high-pitched voice say, "I'll peel you—and then I'll *eat* you!" That was enough for Harry, he turned and ran out of the house as though chased by the Hounds of Hell.

In went Dick, trembling in every limb, and when he reached the foot of the stairs he also heard this unearthly, high-pitched voice saying, "I'll peel you—and then I'll *eat* you!" Dick, brave though he was, turned with a yelp and hurtled back out into the night and the storm.

Tom squared his shoulders, marched in—and turned on

the hall light. And there, at the top of the stairs, was a small boy eating a large bunch of bananas and saying, "I'll peel you—and then I'll *eat* you!"

Tom, Dick, and Harry were unfortunate enough to be captured in the desert by a band of Bedouin Arabs. They were relieved of all their valuables and informed by the chief of the robber band that they were to be executed by a firing-squad at dawn. During the night the three captives discussed how they might get out of their predicament. "I've heard," said Tom, "that Bedouin Arabs are terrified of natural disasters—they think natural disasters are the punishment of God. That might just save us."

Came the dawn, and Tom was facing the firing-squad. Just as the robber chief was about to give the signal to shoot, Tom looked over their heads and shouted, "A sandstorm!"

Immediately there was confusion and panic, and Tom made good his escape. But the next morning saw Dick also facing the firing-squad, and just as the Bedouin chief was about to give the signal to shoot, Dick looked to the right and shouted, "Flood!" Immediately there was further confusion and panic, and Dick also made good his escape.

But the following morning found Harry facing the firing-squad, and just as the firing-squad was awaiting the signal to shoot, Harry looked to the left and shouted, "Fire . . . !"

Tom, Dick, and Harry went out for a walk in the country. They were passing over a very high road bridge when Tom looked down and said, "Look at those wonderful cows! Aren't they splendid? They're English cows, of course!"

"Oh, no, they're not," said Harry. "They're Irish cows. Marvelous beasts—Irish, of course. Anyone can see that."

"You're both wrong," said Dick. "They must be Scottish cows."

"Why must they be Scottish cows?" asked Tom and Harry.

"Because you can see they're carrying their bagpipes!"

Tom, Dick, and Harry were playing croquet, and Harry hit his ball into a clump of bushes. When Dick ran to retrieve the ball Tom said, "Be careful when you go in those bushes, because there's a terrible ghost with one black eye who haunts them!"

Dick refused to believe Tom's story, and bravely ran to the bushes. But inside the bushes all seemed dark and cold and sinister, and to his horror Dick heard a harsh voice say, "I am the ghost with one black eye! If you don't get away from my bushes I will haunt you for the rest of your life!" With a yelp Dick hurtled back to the lawn and told Harry what had happened.

Harry just laughed and said, "You must have been imagining things. You wait there and I'll get the ball."

But when he entered the clump of bushes he also heard

a voice which made his hair rise in terror. "I am the ghost with one black eye!" it said. "And if you don't get away from my bushes I will haunt you for the rest of your life!" And with a scream Harry also tore back to the lawn.

Whereupon Tom went into the clump of bushes, and he also heard the awful, moaning voice saying, "I am the ghost with one black eye! If you don't get away from my bushes I will haunt you for the rest of your life!"

To which Tom replied, "And if you don't give me back that ball you'll be the ghost with two black eyes!"

Tom, Dick, and Harry were in an airplane which was on fire and about to crash. No one aboard had a parachute, so there was nothing for it but to jump out—from five thousand feet! Tom, as he jumped, said, "God save me!" and he landed safely in a haystack. Dick, as he jumped, said, "God save me!" and he landed safely in another haystack. But Harry didn't speak English very well, and as he jumped he said, "God shave me!"—and landed in a barber shop.

Tom, Dick, and Harry were stranded on a desert island. There was nothing to eat and all they had to drink was a bottle of wine, so very naturally they decided to wait as long as possible and then have one third of the bottle each. But the morning after the life-giving bottle had been found, Tom and Dick were appalled to find it empty!

"Where did the wine go?" they demanded angrily of Harry.

"Well, I wanted to drink my share," he replied reasonably, "but as my third was at the bottom I had to drink through yours to get to it!"

While out for a walk one day, Tom, Dick, and Harry came across a wishing well. Above the wishing well was a sign: "Drop In a Penny for Good Luck." So Tom dropped in a penny, made a wish, and walked on; Dick also dropped in a penny, made a wish, and walked on. Harry dropped in a nickel—and waited for his change!

Ghost Gags

What do ghosts eat for dinner?
  Spook-etti.

What do shortsighted ghosts wear?
  Spook-tacles.

What did the Mommy Ghost say to the Baby Ghost?
  "Spook when you're spooken to."

What do you call a drunken ghost?
  A methylated spirit.

Why couldn't the skeleton go to the ball?
  'Cause he had nobody to go with.

What do you do if you see a skeleton running across a busy road?
  Jump out of your skin and join him.

What do ghosts wear in the rain?
  Boo-oots and ghoul-oshes.

What do ghosts eat for breakfast?
  Dreaded wheat.

Why do ghosts like tall buildings?
  'Cause they have lots of scarecases.

What did the ghost guard say?
  "Who ghosts there?"

What do baby ghosts like chewing?
  Booble gum.

What did the baby ghost say when he wanted his favorite food?
   "I scream."

What did one ghost say to the other ghost?
   "I simply do not believe in people."

Where do witches live by the sea?
   Sand-witch.

Why do witches fly about on broomsticks?
   Because vacuum cleaners don't have long enough cords.

What is Dracula's favorite sport?
   Batminton.

What is a ghost's favorite music?
   Haunting melodies.

What job did the lady ghost have on an airplane?
   An air ghostess.

Where do ghosts like to swim?
  In the Dead Sea.

Why was the Mommy Ghost worried about Baby Ghost?
  'Cause he was always in good spirits.

What is the ghosts' favorite Western Town?
  Tombstone.

What do ghosts like to ride on at the fair?
  The Roller Ghoaster.

Where do ghosts live?
  In a far distant terror-tory.

What is the ghosts' favorite stretch of water?
  Lake Erie.

Was Dracula ever married?
  No, he was a bat-chelor.

How does a ghost count?

    One *Boo* Three Four Five Six Seven *Hate* Nine Frighten!

What did the Hungarian ghost have for lunch?

    Ghoulash.

Why did the ghost go to the astrologer?

    'Cause he wanted to see his horrorscope.

Why are ghosts cowards?

    'Cause they've got no guts.

What does the Indian ghost live in?

    A creepy teepee.

When the man ghost met the lady ghost was it love at first fright?

Who brings the Monsters their babies?

    Frankenstork.

How do ghosts get through locked doors?
   They use skeleton keys.

What shows do ghosts like to go to?
   Phantomines.

Where does Dracula always stay when he's in New York?
   In the Vampire State Building.

What do you think of Dracula films?
   Fangtastic!

What does a ghost take for a bad cold?
   Coffin drops.

What are a ghoul's best friend?
   Demons.

Groaners

What goes black and white and black and white and black and white and black and white . . . ?

A penguin rolling down a hill.

What goes white and black and white and black and white and black and white and black . . . ?

A nun rolling down a hill.

What is gray and has four legs and a trunk?

A mouse going on vacation.

Did you hear about the dog which sat down to gnaw a bone?

When it got up it only had three legs . . .

If a flea and a fly pass each other, what time is it?
    Fly past flea.

Why did the man take a pencil to bed?
    To draw the curtains . . . I'd tell you another joke about a pencil but it doesn't have a point.

What happened when a man bought a paper shop?
    It blew away.

What time did the Chinaman go to the dentist?
    Two-thirty. (Tooth hurtee)

Why did the burglar take a shower?
    He wanted to make a clean getaway.

What's stupid and yellow?
    Thick custard.

What's big and yellow and eats rocks?
    A big yellow rock eater.

What would you see at a chicken show?
  Hentertainment.

How do you stop a rooster crowing on Sunday?
  Cook him on Saturday.

Why do idiots eat biscuits?
  Because they're crackers.

What is striped and goes 'round and 'round?
  A zebra in a revolving door.

What is green and hairy and goes up and down?
  A gooseberry in an elevator.

Where was King Solomon's Temple?
  On his forehead.

What do you call an American drawing?
  A Yankee Doodle.

What party game did Jekyll like best?
    Hyde and Seek.

What's tall and smells nice?
    A giraff-odil.

What dance do ducks prefer?
    A quackstep.

Why do bears wear fur coats?
    They'd look silly in plastic raincoats.

If all the cars in Britain were pink, what would you have?
    A car-nation.

What is brown, has four feet, a hump and is found in Alaska?
    A lost camel.

Where are whales weighed?
    At a whale weigh station.

Why did the maniac burn his jacket?
   'Cause he wanted a blazer.

What noise does a cat make on a highway?
   MEOWWWW!

Why did Tiny Tim throw the butter out of the window?
   'Cause he wanted to see a butterfly.

Why did the surveyor take his ruler to bed?
   'Cause he wanted to see how long he would sleep.

Why do cows have horns?
   'Cause their bells don't work.

Have you heard the joke about the garbage truck?
   It's a load of rubbish.

Have you heard the joke about the wall?
   I'd better not tell you—you might not get over it.

Have you heard the joke about the butter?
 I'd better not tell you—you might spread it around.

What is the largest mouse in the world?
 A hippopota-mouse.

What do you call an Eskimo wearing ear muffs and a crash helmet?
 Anything you like—he can't hear a thing.

What do cannibals eat for breakfast?
 Buttered host.

What did the policeman say to the three-headed man?
 "Hello, hello, hello!"

What did the German say to the broken clock?
 "Ve haff vays off makink you tock!"

If a buttercup is yellow, what color is a hiccup?
 Burple.

What do you give a pig with a sore nose?
   Oinkment.

What lies at the bottom of the sea and shivers?
   A nervous wreck.

What is the opposite of minimum?
   Minidad.

What is hairy and coughs?
   A coconut with a cold.

What game do horses like?
   Stable-tennis.

What do you get if a cat swallows a ball of wool?
   Mittens.

Where does a general keep his armies?
   Up his sleevies.

What did the German policeman say to his chest?
  "You're under a-vest!"

Why is there always a wall around a graveyard?
  'Cause people are dying to get in.

If a man was born in Australia, worked in America and died in Europe, what is he?
  Dead.

What did one wall say to the other wall?
  "I'll meet you around the corner."

What do you get if you run over a canary with a lawn mower?
  Shredded tweet.

What was the police dog's telephone number?
  Canine, Canine, Canine.

What do you get if you pour boiling water down a rabbit hole?

   Hot Cross Bunnies.

What do you call a foreign body on a griddle?

   An Unidentified Frying Object.

When is it bad luck to be followed by a black cat?

   When you're a mouse.

How did the exhausted sparrow land safely?

   By sparrowchute.

What roll wanted to rule the world?

   Attila the Bun.

Which King of England invented the fireplace?

   Henry the Grate.

What was purple and wanted to rule the world?

   Alexander the Grape.

What are the best things to put in a fruit pie?
  Your teeth!

What do you call an astronaut's watch?
  A lunar-tick.

When does an astronaut have his midday meal?
  At launch time.

What do you call a mad spaceman?
  An astronut.

How did Noah see to the animals in the Ark?
  By flood-lighting.

What swings through trees and is very dangerous?
  A chimpanzee with a machine gun.

What's green and holds up a stagecoach?
  Jesse Gherkin.

What lives under the sea and carries 64 people?
   An octobus.

What's blue and yellow and has a wing span of 14 yards?
   A two and a half ton parakeet.

What do you call a bald-headed smiler?
   Yul Grynner.

What kind of meringues repeat?
   Boo-meringues.

What has four legs, a tail, whiskers, and flies?
   A dead cat.

What wobbles when it flies?
   A jellycopter

What did the mayonnaise say to the fridge?
   "Close the door—I m dressing."

What are spiders' webs good for?
  Spiders.

What did the rock pool say to another rock pool?
  "Show us your mussels."

Who invented gunpowder?
  A lady who wanted guns to look pretty.

Who was the first underwater spy?
  James Pond.

What do you get when you eat foam?
  Soft in the head.

Did you hear the joke about the field of corn that was 100 feet high?
  You wouldn't like it—it's a very tall story.

In a fight between a hedgehog and a fox, who won?
    The hedgehog won on points.

*What did the Daddy Hedgehog say to his son as he was
about to spank him?*
    "This is going to hurt me far more than it will you..."

What travels 100 miles per hour underground?
    A mole on a motor-bike.

How do you milk a mouse?
    You can't—the bucket won't fit under it.

What is the worst kind of weather for rats and mice?
    When it's raining cats and dogs.

What's worse than raining cats and dogs?
    Hailing taxis.

What do you get when you jump in the Red Sea?
    Wet.

What do you call a cat who swallowed a duck?
  A duck-filled fatty puss.

What's black and white and red all over?
  A sunburned penguin.

Did you hear about the Irish caterpillar?
  It turned into a frog.

What goes in black and comes out white?
  A miller's boot.

Why is the sand wet?
  Because the seaweed.

Why did the Red Indian put a bucket over his head?
  'Cause he wanted to be a pailface.

How do frogs and rabbits make beer?
  I don't know, but they start with hops.

What's seven feet high, green and sits in the corner?
   The Incredible Sulk.

When is the best time to go to bed?
   When the bed won't come to you.

What's brown and white and yellow and goes at 125 miles per hour?
   A train-driver's egg sandwich.

What goes in pink and comes out blue?
   A swimmer on a cold day.

Why did Nelson wear a three-cornered hat?
   To keep his three-cornered head warm.

What was Nelson's baby brother called?
   Half-Nelson.

What's the best way to catch a squirrel?
   Hang upside down from a tree and look like a nut.

What insect is musical?
   A humbug.

What is a cloak?
   The mating call of a Chinese frog.

What goes dot-dot-croak, croak-dot-croak, dot-croak-dot-croak?
   Morse toad.

What are frogs' favorite tales?
   Croak and dagger stories.

Where do tadpoles change into frogs?
   In the croakroom.

What did the plug say to the wall?
   "Socket to me, baby!"

How do you make a thin guinea pig fat?
   Throw him off a cliff and he'll come down "plump!"

What is woolly, covered in chocolate and goes around the sun?
    A Mars Baaaa!

How do you make a cigarette lighter?
    Take the tobacco out.

Why did the owl make everyone laugh?
    'Cause he was a hoot!

How would you avoid starvation on a desert island?
    By eating the sand-which is there.

Where does satisfaction come from?
    A satis-factory.

Do you know the joke about the rope?
    Aw, skip it . . .

Do you know the joke about the two-ton doughnut?
    It takes some swallowing.

Do you know the joke about the bed?
  It hasn't been made yet.

Do you know the joke about the dirty window?
  You wouldn't see through it.

Do you know the joke about the umbrella?
  It'd be over your head.

Do you know how to make a bandstand?
  Take away their chairs.

Which animal is always laughing?
  A happy-potamus.

What do you do if you split your sides laughing?
  Run till you get a stitch.

*What goes A B C D E F G H I J K L M N O P Q
R S T U V W X Y Z slurp?*
  A man eating alphabet soup.

What is the best thing to take into the desert?
   A thirst-aid kit.

Where will you always find diamonds?
   In a pack of cards.

What do you call someone who has a dictionary in his back pocket?
   Smarty pants.

What did the blackbird say to the scarecrow?
   "I'll knock the stuffing out of you."

What did the strawberry say to the second strawberry?
   "However did we get into this jam?"

What did the magnet say to the second magnet?
   "You're very attractive."

What did the tap say to the washer?
   "You're a big drip."

What did the spider say to the beetle?
  "Stop bugging me."

What did the tie say to the hat?
  "You go on ahead and I'll hang around."

What did the invisible man say to his girlfriend?
  "Baby, you're outta sight!"

What did the picture say to the wall?
  "I've got you covered."

What did the cork say to the bottle?
  "If you don't behave I'll plug you."

What was Noah's profession?
  He was an Ark-itect.

What did Cinderella say when the developer mislaid her photographs?
  "Some day my prints will come."

What is a common illness in China?
  Kung Flu.

Where do they go dancing in California?
  San Frandisco.

What do jelly babies wear on their feet?
  Gum boots.

What did the puddle say to the rain?
  "Drop in sometime."

What do you call a baby whale?
  A little squirt.

Why does Batman search for worms?
  To feed his Robin.

What do ducks like on television?
  Duckumentaries.

What famous detective liked to take bubble baths?
  Sherlock Foams.

How does an octopus go into battle?
  Fully armed.

What has one horn and gives milk?
  A milk delivery van.

Why did the tap run?
  'Cause it saw the kitchen sink.

What happened when the glow-worm got trampled on?
  He was de-lighted.

Why did the cracker cry?
  'Cause his mother was a wafer so long.

What did one Egyptian say to the other Egyptian?
  "I can't remember your name but your fez is familiar."

What do you get if you dial
49783446723557463928374627
   A blister on your finger.

Why does the giraffe have a long neck?
   'Cause he can't stand the smell of his feet.

What do mermaids eat for breakfast?
   Merma-lade on toast.

What goes cluck-cluck bang?
   A chicken in a minefield.

What goes ha-ha-ha clonk?
   A man laughing his head off.

What is red, has bumps and a horse, and lives on the prairie?
   The Lone Raspberry.

What is pretty, has big teeth and flies?
   A killer butterfly.

What did the Pink Panther say when he stepped on the ant?

(Sing "Pink Panther" tune) "Dead-ant, dead-ant, dead-ant-dead-ant-dead-ant . . ."

What did the Lone Ranger say when he went to drop off his garbage?

"To-de-dump, to-de-dump, to-de-dump-dump-dump . . ."

What did Batman's mother say when she wanted to call him for lunch?

(*Sing*) "Dinner-dinner-dinner-dinner, dinner-dinner-dinner-dinner, BATMAN!"

Which chestnut invaded Britain?

William the Conker.

What did one tonsil say to the other tonsil?

"Get dressed—the doctor's taking us out tonight."

What do you eat somewhere over the rainbow?

Way up pie. (Way up high.)

What's yellow on the inside and green on the outside?
    A banana disguised as a cucumber.

Where does a dog go when he loses his tail?
    To a re-tailer.

What goes tick-tick woof-woof?
    A watchdog.

Where do cows go on vacation?
    Moo York.

What does a ball do when it stops rolling?
    Looks 'round.

What dog has no tail?
    A hotdog.

What must you be careful not to do when it's raining cats and dogs?
    Step in a poodle.

What happened to the plastic surgeon when he stood by the fire?

He melted.

Now you see it, now you don't—what is it?

A black cat walking over a zebra crossing.

How do you get two whales in a VW bug?

Drive down the highway. (Two whales = to Wales!)

What can't you do if you put 250 melons in the fridge?

Shut the door.

Why did the farmer drive over his potato field with a steam-roller?

'Cause he wanted mashed potatoes.

What did the big candle say to the little candle?

"You're too young to go out."

What is yellow and flickers?

A lemon with a loose connection.

What do you call an 800 pound grizzly bear with a bad temper?
    Sir.

What is the most common illness in birds?
    Flu.

What exams are horses good at?
    S. Hay T.'s.

What do you call a sleeping bull?
    A bulldozer.

What flour do elves use?
    Elf-raising flour.

What's white and goes up?
    A stupid snowflake.

Did you hear about the car with the wooden engine and the wooden wheels?
    It wooden go.

What's round and bad-tempered?
   A vicious circle.

Where do gnomes live?
   Gnome Sweet Gnome.

What do you do with a sick parakeet?
   Give him tweetment.

What is long, has a red hat and lies in a box?
   A match.

What do lady sheep wear?
   Ewe-niforms.

Happy Families
or blood is thicker than water— but who wants to be that thick?

"How old is your Grandad?
  "I don't know, but we've had him a long time."

"There were fifteen of us kids when I was a youngster."
  "Fifteen! That's a big family."
  "It sure is. There were so many diapers hanging up we had a rainbow in the hall."

"One day my Mom sent my Dad into the garden to cut a cabbage for our dinner. Dad took out his knife, bent down— his hand slipped and he cut his throat!"
  "Golly! What did your Mom do?"
  "Opened up a can of peas."

"I'm divorcing my wife for smoking in bed."
    "That doesn't sound all that serious."
    "Oh, she doesn't smoke cigarettes."
    "What does she smoke, then?"
    "Bacon."

It didn't take long to wind up Grandad's estate. All he
left was a cuckoo clock.

"Will you love me when I'm old and ugly?"
    "Darling, of course I do."

"We never wanted for anything when I was a kid."
    "That's nice."
    "All except my Uncle Colin, that is. He was wanted
for burglary."

When Mr. Maxwell's wife left him he couldn't sleep. She
took the bed.

"Grandad, is it fun being ninety-nine?"

"Certainly it is. If I wasn't ninety-nine I'd be dead."

The housewife answered a knock on the door and found a total stranger standing on the step. "Excuse me for disturbing you, madam," he said politely, "but I pass your house every morning on my way to work, and I've noticed that every day you appear to be hitting your son on the head with a loaf of bread."

"That's right."

"Every day you hit him on the head with a loaf of bread, and yet this morning you were clouting him with a chocolate cake ... ?"

"Well, today's his birthday."

It is truly said that children brighten a home—they never turn the lights off.

Jack met Claud in the street and noticed that Claud was carrying a small parcel.

"Been shopping then, Claud?" he asked.

"Yes," replied Claud, "I've just been to the perfumery to buy a present for the wife's birthday tomorrow."

"Oh, yes?" said Jack, "what did you get her, then?"

"A bottle of toilet water. Very expensive—this little bottle cost me twenty-five dollars!'

"Twenty-five dollars for a bottle of toilet water?!" said Jack in amazement. "Why don't you come home with me? You can have all you want for nothing!"

"I forgot my sister's birthday."
"Gosh! What did she say?"
"Nothing... for six weeks."

The son of a businessman had agreed to join the family business, and on his very first day at the factory his father took him on to the roof and said, "Now, my son, I am about to give you your first lesson in business. Stand on the edge of the roof."

"On the edge, Dad?" said the puzzled youth.

"On the very edge."

"Very well, Dad," and the obedient son did as he was told.

"Now, when I say 'Jump!' said his father, "I want you to jump."

"But it's a twenty foot drop!"

"My boy," said the father, "you want to learn the business, don't you?"

"Yes, Dad."

"And you trust me?"

"Yes, Dad."

"Right. Then do as I say—Jump!"

And the boy jumped, only to crash painfully to the ground twenty feet below. His father ran down the stairs to where the youth was lying bruised, battered, and winded.

"Now, my son," said his father, "you have just learned your first lesson in business—*never trust anybody*!"

Mrs. McLean had such an ugly baby she didn't push the stroller—she pulled it.

"I don't think my Mom knows much about children."

"Why do you say that?"

"Because she always puts me to bed when I'm wide awake and gets me up when I'm sleepy."

"I hear you've got a new baby sister," said Jonathan to his friend William.

"Yeah."

"Is she fun to play with?"

"Nah."

"Well, why don't you change her?"

"We can't," explained William, "we've used her a week already."

Where does a goose come from?

A gooseberry bush.

The neighbor was congratulating Mrs. Smith on the arrival of her new baby. "And I bet your Peter's pleased," she said, referring to Mrs. Smith's six-year-old son.

"Oh yes, he is," replied the new mother, "now he can stop teasing the cat."

Father's Day is just like Mother's Day only you don't have to spend as much...

It was local election time and the candidate was visiting all the houses in his area. At one house the door was answered by a small boy. "Tell me, young man," said the politician, "is your Mommy in the Republican Party or the Democratic Party?"

"Neither," said the imp, "she's in the bathroom."

Old Granny Parkinson had won over half a million dollars in the lottery, but as she was a frail little woman her family was concerned that the shock of hearing the news might prove too much for her. Accordingly, they called in the family doctor to ask his advice. "I'll tell her if you like," said the doctor. "I'll lead up to it gradually." The family accepted his offer gratefully, and showed him into the old lady's bedroom. The doctor pretended to give her a routine examination and then began to chat generally of this and that, carefully leading the conversation 'round to money.

"Tell me Mrs. Parkinson," he said, "what would you do if you suddenly came into half a million dollars?"

"Half a million?" said the old lady reflectively, "well,

you've always been very good to me, doctor, so I think I'd give half of it to you."

And the doctor immediately collapsed and died of shock.

"Mom, can I have a quarter for being good?"

"All right, but I wish you could be good-for-nothing!"

Little Jackie's mother was on the telephone with the boy's dentist. "I don't understand it," she complained, "I thought his treatment would only cost $20, but you have charged me $80."

"It is usually $20, madam," agreed the dentist, "but Jackie yelled so loudly that three of my other patients ran away!"

"Mom, can I go out and play?"

"What, in those clothes?"

"No—in the park."

Alfie had been listening to his sister practicing her singing. "Sis," he said, "I wish you'd sing Christmas carols."

"That's nice of you, Alfie," she said. "Why?"

"Then I'd only have to hear you once a year!"

One small boy was telling his friend about the mysteries of his big sister's makeup. "She's worried about what she calls her 'complexion,'" he said, "so she puts lemon juice on her face."

"Lemon juice!?" exclaimed his pal. "No wonder she always looks so sour!"

"Louisa," asked her small brother, "can you help me with my math homework?"

"Certainly not," replied Louisa indignantly. "It wouldn't be right."

"Maybe not," said the boy, "but you could at least try . . . !"

Julian was the most advanced boy in his class. He sat in the front.

"My sister's taking cooking lessons," said little Nick. "Last night she made some soup—ugh!—it was awful. This morning some pygmies came over from Africa to dip their darts into it . . . and for lunch today she gave us cold boiled ham. That's ham boiled in cold water."

"My Dad," said the vain girl loftily, "says that when I grow up I'll be a raving beauty."

"Why?" asked her catty friend. "Is he going to put you in a lunatic asylum?"

"Certainly not! He says I'm sure to have lots of men at my feet."

"Very likely—podiatrists!"

"Hello, Ginger!" her brother called cheerily to his sister.

"Don't call me Ginger!" she snapped furiously. "My hair is the color of gold."

"Yeah," he replied with a jeer, "twenty-two carrots!"

The welfare worker was paying his first visit to a problem family in his area, and the door was opened by a small girl.

"Whaddy want?" she asked suspiciously.

"Is your mother in?" asked the welfare officer.

"Nah," answered the child, "she's in a loony bin, ain't she?"

"Oh . . . well, is your father in?"

"Nah. He's in prison, ain't he?"

"Oh dear . . . what about your brother?"

"He's in reform school."

"Good gracious. Is there a big sister looking after you, then?"

"She was until last week but now she's at Harvard University."

"Your mother's in an asylum, your father's in prison, your brother's in reform school and your sister's at college?"

"That's right."

"What is she studying?"

"She ain't. They're studyin' her!"

Cliff had just formed his own rock 'n' roll band, and his little brother said one day, "Cliff, I wish you and your band could be on TV!"

"You think we're good, eh?"

"Then I could turn you off!"

"My sister just got engaged to an Irish guy."

"Oh, really?"

"No—O'Reilly!"

"What are you learning at school now, Brenda?" asked her Granny.

"French, German, and we've just started Algebra."

"Really?" said the old lady, impressed. "I used to learn French and German but I've never heard anyone speak Algebra."

"Dad, the career counselor said that with a mind like mine I should study criminal law."

"That's wonderful, son. I'm proud of you."

"He said I had a criminal mind."

"So," thundered Stanley's furious father, "you've been expelled from college, have you?"

"Yes, Dad. I am a fugitive from a brain gang."

"I saw you kissing my sister last night!" jeered the brat to the embarrassed teenager.

"All right, all right! Not so loud," said the youth. "Here's fifty cents to keep your mouth shut."

"Gee, thanks! Wait a minute and I'll give you twenty cents change."

"Twenty cents change? What for?"

"I like to be fair," said the youngster, "and it's the same price for everybody!"

Rebecca's mother found her in her bedroom in floods of tears. "What on earth is the matter, dear?" she inquired anxiously.

"I've just had a letter from my boyfriend," sobbed the distraught girl, "and he's only put two kisses on the bottom!"

"So?"

"I hate being double-crossed!"

Alan had just asked his father for an increase in his allowance.

"What do you want more money for?" demanded his father.

"Well, I'm thirteen now, Dad," explained the lad, "and I'm thinking of going out with girls."

"Girls? What kind of girls?"

"Girls with money."

"Mom, now that I'm fifteen, can I wear lipstick and mascara and perfume and pluck my eyebrows and get my hair waved?"

"No, James, you may not."

"How are you getting on with your football, Peter?"

"Well, Dad, pretty good. The coach said I was one of the team's greatest drawbacks!"

At a party the old lady was bemoaning the behavior of the youth of today. "Look at the girl over there," she complained. "I don't know what young girls are coming to! She's wearing boy's jeans, a boy's shirt, and that haircut is so boyish—you wouldn't know she was a girl at all, would you?"

"Well, as it happens, I would," came the reply, "because she is my daughter."

"Oh dear," said the old lady embarrassed, "I'm so sorry—I didn't know you were her father."

"I'm not. I'm her mother."

The eldest of six boys had just passed his driving test. His brothers gathered around enviously to congratulate him, to which he replied graciously, "Thanks, boys. And I tell you what: now that I've got my own car, you can all move up one bike!"

"Larry! Come here!" said his furious mother, putting the telephone down. "I've just had a call from Mrs. Harrison about your behavior to her Doris at the school dance last night. You wretched, rude boy!"

"I was nice to her, Mom, really I was!" protested the youth. "I even paid her a compliment when we had a dance."

"Did you, indeed?" said his mother grimly. "And what exactly did you say?"

"I said, 'Gosh, Doris, you sweat less than any fat girl I've ever danced with!'"

"Daddy, do you think I'm vain?"

"Vain, dear? No, I wouldn't say so. Why do you ask?"

"Because most girls as pretty as me are."

"You stupid girl!" said her mother crossly, "didn't I tell you to watch that saucepan and notice when it boiled over?"

"But I did, Mom. It was half-past ten."

"I've made the chicken soup for lunch today," said big sister proudly to her small brother.

"Thank goodness for that," said the boy, "I thought it was for us."

SISTER: "Try some of my sponge cake."
BROTHER: (*Nibbling on a piece*) "It's a bit tough, isn't it?"
SISTER: "Yes, I can't understand it. I bought the sponge fresh from the drug store this morning!"

BROTHER: "You've just backed the car over my bike!"
SISTER: "Serves you right. You shouldn't leave it in the hall."

Russell couldn't swim, yet when he fell into the river and was floundering around desperately, what did his callous friend say from the safety of the bank? "Russell—if you don't come up for the third time, can I have your sheath knife?"

Susannah was watching her big sister covering her face with cream. "What's that for?" she asked.

"To make me beautiful," came the reply. Susannah watched in silence as her sister then wiped her face clean.

"Doesn't work, does it?" was the little girl's comment.

Harold's big sister was almost in tears over her cooking. "I don't know what to do," she moaned, looking at yet another unsuccessful batch of cakes. "What can I do to make my cakes light?"

"I tell you what, Sis," said Harold helpfully, "why not soak them in kerosene!"

"Are you from a large family?"

"Yes, I'm the fourteenth of thirteen children."

"Are you married?"

"Yes."

"Children?"

"Three boys and six girls."

"That's nine altogether."

"No—one at a time."

"My boyfriend," said Miss Vanity, on her nineteenth birthday, "says I have a skin like a peach!"

"Is that so?" said her insolent little brother. "And who wants to look like a nineteen-year-old peach . . . ?!"

"What would you like for your birthday, Sis?"

"I'd like a dress to match the color of my eyes."

"Would you? Where am I going to get a bloodshot dress?"

"My boyfriend says I look like a gorgeous Italian!" said Miss Conceited.

"He's right," said her brother.

"Sophia Loren?"

"No—spaghetti!"

"Is my dinner hot?" asked the excessively late husband.

"It should be," said his furious wife, "it's been on the fire since seven o'clock!"

"I think it's true when they say television causes violence," said the small boy.

"What makes you think that?"

"'Cause every time I switch it on my Dad hits me."

The insurance salesman was trying to persuade a housewife to take out a life insurance policy. "Now supposing your husband were to die," he said, "what would you get?"

"Oh, a Labrador, I think," replied the housewife. "They're always good company!"

"Now, Sam," said the wife to her rather uncouth husband, "we've got company coming to tea on Sunday, so I want you on your best behavior."

"What do you mean, woman?" demanded the aggrieved husband.

"Well, for a start, I don't want you drinking your tea out of the saucer like you usually do."

"Then what shall I drink it out of?"

"Out of the cup, of course!" said his wife, exasperated.

"Out of the cup? But if I do that I'll get the spoon in my eye!"

Damien was being severely scolded by his father for fighting. "Now, Damien," said his angry parent, "this will not do! You must learn that you can't have everything you want in this life. There must always be give and take."

"But there was, Dad!" protested the aggressive youngster. "I gave him a black eye and took the apple!"

"Eat up all your spinach, Jemima. It'll put color in your cheeks."

"But who wants to have green cheeks?"

"Last night my sister fell out of her bedroom window."

"Golly! Did she hurt herself?"

"No—we live on the first floor."

"Donovan! How many more times will I have to tell you? Don't eat with your knife!"

"But, Mom! My fork's got a leak!"

"Dad, there's a man at the door collecting for the new swimming pool."

"Give him a glass of water!"

"Mom! All the kids at school call me Bighead!"

"Never mind what those stupid children say, dear. Now, go to the grocery and get me five pounds of potatoes in your cap."

"When I was a lad," said Grandpa, "all the railway trains were steam-powered."

"Really, Grandpa?" said his wide-eyed grandchild. "Does that mean they were in black and white?"

Here and There

Margaret was telling her friend about her vacation abroad. "When we got to the airport," she said, "there was this man outside yelling 'It's wrong to fly! It's against nature! If God had meant us to fly he'd have given us wings.'"

"Who was he?" asked her friend.

"The pilot!"

Some people are terrified of flying. Take poor old Royston, who wanted to go to Spain for his summer holiday; nothing would induce him to go on a plane so he had to travel by boat and train. But he was out of luck—his train crashed. A plane fell on it . . .

The traveling salesman had booked himself in for the night in a small boarding house, but due to a lengthy business meeting he didn't arrive until after midnight. He could see no signs of life, but not wanting to spend the night on the

116

doorstep he pressed the bell. After an interval an upstairs window opened and an angry woman in dressing-gown and curlers peered out. "What is it?" she demanded.

"It's Mr. Jenkins," replied the hapless salesman, "I'm staying here."

"All right," came the response. "Stay there." And she slammed down the window!

At a small country railway station the ticket clerk-cum-porter noticed a stranger, who had just alighted from one of the infrequent trains that stopped there, examining a timetable.

"Excuse me, sir" he asked, "are you lost?"

"Certainly not," said the traveler, "I'm here. It's your station that's lost!"

Two friends were having a cup of coffee in a diner at Grand Central Station.

"Do you know," said one, "I once went from here to Brooklyn and it didn't cost me a penny!"

"How was that?" asked the second.

"I walked."

"I think we just got a flat tire."

"How did that happen?"

"There was a fork in the road!"

The great Explorer claimed to have spent a whole year in the deepest jungles of Central Africa. "After my supplies ran out," he declared, "I lived on nothing but snake and pygmy pie..."

"I flew to Germany last year."
   "So did I."
   "Doesn't it make your arms tired!?"

"Hey, cabby! How much to take me to the station?"
   "Five bucks, sir."
   "And how much for my suitcase?"
   "No charge for the suitcase, sir."
   "Okay. Take the case and I'll walk."

"I've never flown before," said the nervous old lady to the pilot. "You will bring me down safely, won't you?"
   "All I can say, ma'am," said the pilot, "is that I've never left anyone up there yet!"

"Once when I was shipwrecked," said the teller of tall tales, "I lived on a can of sardines for a week!"
   "Really?" yawned a bored listener, "I'm surprised you didn't fall off."

The school group was assembled for a day trip to Nantucket. "Harris," said the principal, "we must all be very careful on the ferry ride. If one of the boys falls overboard —what do you do?"

"I shout 'boy overboard!,' sir."

"Good. And what do you do if a teacher falls overboard?"

"Er—which one, sir?"

On board the liner in mid-Atlantic a nervous passenger was being comforted by a steward. "There's nothing to worry about, ma'am," he said soothingly. "After all, we're only two miles from land."

"Only two miles?"

"Yes. Straight down!"

"I hope this plane doesn't travel faster than sound," said the old lady to the stewardess.

"Why?"

"Because my friend and I want to talk, that's why."

Charlie always takes his vacation in March. He says he likes to get in early while the sheets are still clean...

"I tried surf-riding while I was in Australia."

"How did you do?"

"Not very well. I couldn't get the horse near the water."

It was an extremely rough English Channel crossing from Weymouth to Jersey, and one wretched green-faced passenger was hugging the rail when a steward approached him.

"Lunch, sir?" asked the tactless steward.

"No, thanks," groaned the passenger. "Just throw it overboard and save me the trouble..."

Mr. and Mrs. Thorne had just reached the airport in the nick of time to catch the plane for their two week's vacation in Majorca. "I wish we'd brought the piano with us," said Mr. Thorne.

"What on earth for?" asked his wife.

"I've left the tickets on it."

"And on this tour, ladies and gentlemen," explained the guide, "we shall be going where the hand of man has never set foot!"

Heavily encumbered with bags and cases, the would-be passenger hurtled across the station concourse, through the barrier and on to the platform—just in time to see his train pulling out. As he stood there, puffing and panting, with sweat streaming down his reddened face, a sympathetic porter said to him, "Just missed your train, sir?"

"No, you fool," fumed the man. "I didn't like the look of it so I chased it out of the station!"

"When you go on a double-decker bus, do you prefer riding inside or on the top deck?"

"Well, I prefer the top but I find it very difficult to get the horse up the stairs..."

Halfway across the Atlantic Ocean, the captain of the airliner addressed the passengers. "I regret to say, ladies and gentlemen," he announced, "that one of our engines has failed. This puts us in no danger, however, since the aircraft can function perfectly well on the remaining three engines. But it does mean that our arrival in New York will be delayed by one hour. That is all."

A few minutes later a further announcement was made. "I regret to say, ladies and gentlemen," he explained calmly, "that another of our engines has failed. There is still no danger, as this aircraft can function perfectly well on the remaining two engines. But it does mean that our arrival in New York will be delayed by two hours."

Half an hour later the passengers heard their captain yet again. "I regret to say, ladies and gentlemen, that yet another of our engines has failed. There is still no danger whatsoever, as this aircraft can function perfectly well on one engine only. But it does mean that our arrival in New York will be delayed now by three hours."

"I hope the fourth engine doesn't fail as well," said one passenger to another, "or we'll be up here forever!"

Mr. Silly suffered agonies from large bunions on his feet, and his doctor advised him to take a vacation by the sea and soak his feet in salt water. Mr. Silly had never been to the seaside before, and was quite excited by the prospect. He picked a pretty little fishing village in Maine, and on the first morning walked eagerly down to the quayside. And there he saw a fisherman, who was cleaning his nets, hauling a bucket of seawater up on the end of a piece of rope.

Mr. Silly, being rather a silly person as his name implies, thought that the fisherman was selling the seawater, and asked him, "How much is a bucketful?" Now the fisherman was a crafty fellow, and seeing the chance to make some money replied, "Five dollars to you, sir."

"Very well, here you are," said Mr. Silly, handing over the money. The fisherman took it and put the bucket down. Mr. Silly stood in the bucket for half an hour or so, enjoying the sun and the view, and then, after drying his feet and putting his shoes and socks back on, decided to go for a walk. A few hours later he found himself back at the quayside, by which time the tide had gone down and hardly any water was to be seen.

"My goodness!" he said admiringly to the fisherman, "you must have marvelous business here!"

"When I was on vacation at the seaside last year a crab bit off one of my toes!"

"Which one?"

"I don't know—they all look alike to me."

A policeman saw a man dressed as a cowboy in the street, complete with huge Stetson hat, spurs, and six shooters.

"Excuse me, sir," said the policeman, "who are you?"

"My name's Tex, officer," said the cowboy.

"Tex, eh?" said the policeman, "Are you from Texas?"

"Nope. Louisiana."

"Louisiana? So why are you called Tex?"

"Don't want to be called Louise, do I?"

Desmond was making his very first journey by train. He sat goggle-eyed in a corner seat watching the landscape flash past, and laughed with glee as another train went whooshing by. His train then stopped at a signal light and another train went rushing by in the opposite direction.

"Oooh, look, Mom!" he cried, "it came back!"

In Foreign Parts

or do you like being abroad?

"In China," said the returned tourist, "I saw a woman hanging from a tree."

"Shanghai?"

"No, about six feet off the ground."

"Ah'm frae Glasgae," said the Scot.

"Are you, now?" replied the Cockney. "Jus' dahn 'ere ter learn the langwidge, are yer?"

"What do you think of this suit? I had it made in Hong Kong."

"Very nice. But what's that hump on the back?"

"Oh, that's the tailor. He's still working on it."

The newly arrived young Chinese lad from Hong Kong telephoned his brother who was living in Manchester. The young man was speaking in laborious English when his brother interrupted him, saying, "Why don't you speak in Chinese?"

"Oh," said the newcomer, "I didn't know English telephones could speak Chinese!"

An English tourist in a Cairo bazaar was offered a large skull by a street-trader. "Dis de skull of great Queen Cleopatra, my friend," said the Egyptian, "only one hundred English pounds."

"No thank you," said the Englishman. "It's far too expensive."

"How 'bout dis one, my friend?" said the street-trader, producing a small skull.

"Whose skull is that?"

"Dis de skull of great Queen Cleopatra when she was little girl!"

A huge American car screeched to a halt in a sleepy Warwickshire village, and the driver called out to a local inhabitant, "Hey—am I on the right road to Shakespeare's birthplace?"

"Aye, straight on, sir," said the rustic, "but no need to hurry. He's dead."

An Englishwoman just back from the United States was telling her friends about the trip. "When my husband first saw the Grand Canyon, his face dropped a mile," she said.

"Why, was he disappointed with the view?"

"No, he fell over the edge."

"My wife is like the Mona Lisa."

"You mean she's beautiful and has an enigmatic smile?"

"No—she's flat as a canvas and ought to be in a museum."

A new porter in Paris was instructed by the manager that it was important to call the guests by their names, in order to make them feel welcome and that the easiest way to find out their names was to look at their luggage. Armed with this advice, the porter took two guests up to their rooms, put down their bags and said, "I 'ope you 'ave a 'appy stay 'ere in Paris, Mr. and Mrs. Genuine Cow'ide."

A tourist to Ireland was being shown the local beauty spot by a guide. "Ye see them mountains in the distance, sir?"

"Yes," said the visitor.

"Well, sir, them is the highest mountains in the world, sir. All exceptin' them in furren parts, that is."

Notice outside Irish police station:

A REWARD IS OFFERED FOR THE BODY OF

Kevin Laffan

Believed drowned while fishing.
Description: Age 36, height 5 ft. 10 in.
Black hair. Pronounced stutter.

The train was crawling slowly across country from Dublin to Ballinasloe, and the English tourist was growing increasingly impatient. Finally he jumped out at one of the many interminable stops, walked along to the engine driver and said, "Can't you go any faster, driver?"

"Sure I can at that," replied the driver, "but I'm not allowed to leave my train."

The leader of an Irish expedition to scale Mount Everest had returned, and was giving a press conference in Dublin.

"Did you make it to the summit?" asked a reporter.

"No, not quite," said the Irish mountaineer. "We got to within fifty feet of the top, and then we ran out of scaffolding."

At a diplomatic reception the Mexican general appeared in a magnificent uniform, liberally bespattered with medals and decorations. "That's most impressive," said the British ambassador. "Tell me, general, what did you get all those for?"

"In your money," replied the Mexican general, "about £4!"

"What's Norway like?"
"Sweden without matches."

The sweet young lady from Lapland arrived at the English family's house to begin as an *au pair*. "Now, dear," said her English hostess, "I'd like you to make the children's bed in the morning—"

"Oh, excuse me, please, Mrs. Benson, but to make beds—I do not know how."

"Oh," said Mrs. Benson, "well, never mind. You can make the lunch for me and—"

"Oh, excuse me, please, Mrs. Benson, but to cook— I do not know how."

"I see . . . what about cleaning and dusting, then?"

"Cleaning and dusting? I am afraid—"

"You do not know how, yes. Tell me, my dear," said Mrs. Benson through gritted teeth, "what can you do?"

"I can milk a reindeer."

"So you're not going to Berlin this year?"

"No, it's Rome we're not going to. It was Berlin we didn't go to last year."

Two aliens from a flying saucer landed near a small village in Dorset. They walked towards the village, and the first thing they came across was a mail box. "Take me to your leader," said the first alien.

"It's no use talking to him," said the other, "can't you see he's only a child?"

On the doorstep stood a turbanned, brown-skinned figure. "Who are you?" asked the resident.

"I am your new milkman," said the caller.

"Oh, yes? Where are you from?"

"Pakistan."

"Wow—you've got a big round!"

Did you hear about the Russian company of soldiers answering roll call? The sergeant sneezed and six soldiers called out, "Here!"

An English tourist in the west of the United States came across an American Indian lying down with his ear pressed

129

hard on the trail. "What are you listening for?" asked the visitor.

"Stagecoach pass half hour ago," said the brave.

"How can you tell?"

"Broke my neck."

A Yorkshireman on holiday in Spain was taken to see his first bullfight. He watched impassively for a while, and then got to his feet, yelling, "Nay, lad! If you don't hold the red flag still, he'll never run into the damn thing!"

For months the Indian village had been terrorized by a huge man-eating tiger, until they were frightened to go out of their homes at night. Eventually the elders of the village appealed to the Government, and the greatest tiger hunter of them all was dispatched to rid them of the blood-crazed beast.

The great hunter took up a position where tracks of the huge tiger had last been seen, and settled down to wait. On the third night the hunter sensed a stillness, a menace in the jungle; he heard a soft paddling of feet, and sure enough, there through the trees he saw two great glowing eyes coming toward him. By the distance between the eyes he calculated that this must be the largest tiger ever known, and without further ado he took up his trusty gun and fired. Bang!

But still those two red, glowing eyes came toward him! How could he have missed? He immediately fired his second barrel—but still those two red, glowing eyes came toward him . . . he was the finest shot in India, how was it possible that he could have missed again? There was no time to reload and the monstrous tiger was almost upon him. As the beast crouched to spring the great hunter switched on his flashlight—and saw two tigers, each with an eye shut . . .

Commissioned by a zoo to bring them some baboons, the big-game hunter devised a novel scheme to trap them—his only requirements being a sack, a gun, and a particularly vicious and bad-tempered dog.

He tramped into the jungle with his assistant, and after several weeks they finally reached an area where baboons were numerous—though that didn't make them any easier to catch. "This is what we'll do," he explained to his baffled assistant. "I'll climb this tree and shake the branches; if there are any baboons up there they will then fall to the ground—the dog will bite their tails and immobilize them so that you can pick them up quite safely and put them in the sack."

"But what do I need a gun for?" asked the assistant.

"If I should fall out of the tree by mistake, shoot the dog!"

Mr. and Mrs. Shaw were on safari in darkest Africa. They were walking cautiously through the jungle when suddenly a huge lion sprang out in front of them, seized Mrs. Shaw in its jaws and started to drag her off into the bush.

"Shoot!" she screamed to her husband. "Shoot!"

"I can't!" he yelled back, "I've run out of film!"

Irish Stew in the Name of the Law!

What do you get if you dial 116? Three policemen standing on their heads.

"Are you counsel for the defense?"
  "No. I'm the fellow that stole the chickens."

Three men were in court, and the judge, who had a terrible squint, said to the first, "How do you plead?"
  "Not guilty," said the second.
  "I'm not talking to you," snapped the judge.
  "I didn't say a word," said the third.

"I see the police in Liverpool are looking for a man with one eye called Murphy."
  "What's his other eye called?"

"I see the police in Manchester are looking for a man with a hearing aid."

"Why don't they use glasses?"

"What did your father say when you were sent to jail?"

"Hello, son."

POLICEMAN: "I'll have to report you. You were driving at ninety miles an hour."

MOTORIST: "Nonsense, officer. I've only been driving for ten minutes at most."

A country policeman cycling down the lane was astonished to see a hiker walking along bent under the weight of a large wooden sign which read: *To Plymouth*.

"Why are you carrying that?" asked the limb of the law.

"I'm walking to Plymouth," explained the hiker, "and I don't want to lose my way!"

"It's a pity you've gone on a hunger strike," said the convict's wife on visiting day.

"Why?"

"I've put a file in your cake."

POLICEMAN: "You were exceeding the speed limit, ma'am, weren't you?"

LADY MOTORIST: "Yes, I was, sir, but you see my brakes are so bad that I wanted to get home before I had an accident..."

"What is your occupation?" asked the magistrate.

"I'm a locksmith, your honor."

"And what were you doing in the jeweler's shop at three in the morning when the police officers entered?"

"Making a bolt for the door!"

"I knew a man who married his sister."

"That's against the law!"

"No, it isn't. He was a parson."

"I'll have to lock you up for the night," the English policeman told the unruly tourist.

"Lock me up? What's the charge?"

"No charge. It's on Her Majesty."

A man traveling at 130 miles per hour on the interstate was stopped by highway police.

"Sorry, officer," said the driver, "was I driving too fast?"

"No, sir. You were flying too low."

A policeman was escorting a prisoner to jail when his hat blew off. "Shall I run and get it for you?" asked the prisoner obligingly.

"You must think I'm dumb," said the officer. "You stand here and I'll get it."

"What makes you think the prisoner was drunk?" asked the magistrate.

"Well, your honor," replied the arresting officer, "I saw him lift up the manhole cover and walk away with it, and when I asked him what it was for he said, 'I want to listen to it on my record player.'"

"Why do you like being a policeman?"

"Because in my job the customer is never right!"

"Can I help you?" said the telephone operator.

"Yes, get me Interpol. Quick!"

"You'll have to dial the International operator, caller."

"Oh, very well." The caller dialed again.

"International operator. Can I help you?"

"Yes, I want Interpol. Quick. It's important!"

"Do you have the number, caller?"

"No, I don't. But please hurry!"

"You'll have to speak to Directory Assistance in Paris, caller. I'll connect you."

"Thank you. Hurry, please!" There was a longish pause and then a French voice said, "Can I 'elp you, caller?"

"Yes, give me the number of Interpol. And hurry, please, I'm getting desperate!"

"One moment, monsieur . . . the number is Paris 28945."

"Thanks." And he dialed the number frantically.

"Allo?"

"Is that Interpol?"

"Oui, monsieur."

"Thank heavens! Listen—I want to send some flowers to my mother . . . !"

Mr. Smith and Mr. Brown were up before the magistrate for fighting, and Smith was fined $40.

"Forty dollars, your honor?" he said bitterly, "but I was just defending myself—Brown bit half my ear off!"

"And you, Brown," said the magistrate, "are bound to keep the peace for a year."

"Oh, I can't do that, your honor," replied Brown, "I threw it away!"

"Prisoner at the bar, you have pleaded not guilty although no fewer than six people claim to have seen you in the act of stealing the diamonds!"

"That's nothing; I can produce millions who didn't!"

"Guilty or not guilty of begging?" asked the magistrate.

"Nearly guilty," said the beggar.

"What do you mean, 'nearly' guilty?" asked the puzzled magistrate.

"Well, your honor, I asked the lady for fifty cents but I didn't get it."

The trial had been constantly interrupted by heckling in the public gallery, and the judge had had enough. "The next person who interrupts the proceedings will be thrown out of my court!" he said severely, at which the defendant yelled, "Hooray!"

"You are charged with stealing a television set."

"I only took it as a joke, your honor."

"Where did you take it?"

"To Glasgow."

"That's what I'd call taking a joke too far. Your fine is one hundred dollars."

"How did you get on in court yesterday?"

"Oh, fine..."

"Oh don't talk to me about lawyers," sighed the widow. "I've had so much trouble settling my late husband's estate that I sometimes wish he hadn't died..."

"Where are your taillights?" said the traffic cop to the motorist.

The motorist looked around and started. "Never mind my taillights," he said, "where's my trailer?!"

"Did you actually *see* my client bite off his neighbor's nose?" asked the defending counsel.

"Well, I didn't actually see him bite it off," admitted the witness, "but I saw him spit it out!"

"You say you have only one brother?" queried the not-very-alert magistrate. "But your sister has testified that she has two..."

The agitated woman had dialed 911.

"Police, fire, or ambulance?" asked the operator.

"I want a vet!" demanded the panic-stricken woman.

"A vet?" said the emergency service operator in surprise. "What for?"

"To open my bulldog's jaws."

"But why did you call 911?"

"There's a burglar in them."

"Why did you steal that parakeet?"

"For a lark, your honor."

At the police station the drunk was asked his name by the station sergeant.

"John Smith," was the reply.

"Come along now," said the station sergeant wearily, "you can do better than that."

"Oh, all right," said the drunk, "I'm the Prince of Wales."

"That's better," said the policeman, "you can't fool me with that John Smith stuff!"

The police officer was calling up his station on his pocket radio. "I'm outside the Plaza Cinema on High Street," he reported. "A man has been robbed—I've got one of them."

"Which one?"

"The one that was robbed."

"You say your brother hit you over the head with a shovel?"

"That's right—and I want him arrested."

"When was this, sir?"

"Last night."

"You don't show any marks of having been hit with a shovel?"

"You should see the shovel!"

"So it took six policemen to lock you up, I understand?" said the magistrate to the burly prisoner.

"That's right, your honor," he admitted, "but it would only take one to let me out!"

139

"Why have you painted your car red on one side and blue on the other?"

"So that if I bang into anyone the witnesses will have a marvelous time in court contradicting each other!"

"I was thrown in prison once, you know," said the teller of tall tales. "They put me in a cell with my hands tied behind my back. So I put my big toe in the keyhole and gave a mighty jerk. And *snap!*"

"You broke the lock?"

"No, I broke my big toe."

Knock! Knock!

Who's there?
  Little old lady.
  Little old lady who?
  I didn't know you could yodel.

- Who's there?
Amanda.
Amanda who?
Amanda fix the television.

- Who's there?
Waiter.
Waiter who?
Waiter minute while I tie my shoelaces.

- Who's there?
Walrus.
Walrus who?
Why do you walrus ask that silly question?

- Who's there?
Doris.
Doris who?
Doris locked—that's why I knocked.

- Who's there?
Granny. Knock! Knock!
Who's there?
Granny. Knock! Knock!
Who's there?
Granny. Knock! Knock!
Who's there?
Granny. Knock! Knock!
Who's there?
Aunt.
Aunt who?
Aunt you glad Granny's gone?

- Who's there?
Lettuce.
Lettuce who?
Lettuce in, won't you?

- Who's there?
York.
York who?
York coming over to our place.

- Who's there?
Alison.
Alison who?
Alison to my radio in the mornings.

- Who's there?
Isabel.
Isabel who?
Isabel broken, 'cause I had to knock?!

- Ring! Ring!
Who's there?
Hurd my.
Hurd my who?
Hurd my hand so I can't knock.

- Who's there?
Arthur.
Arthur who?
Arthur any biscuits left?

- Who's there?
Ivor.
Ivor who?
Ivor sore hand from knocking on your door!

- Who's there?
Mister.
Mister who?
Mister last bus home.

- Who's there?
Atch.
Atch who?
Nasty cold you've got.

- Who's there?
Doctor.
Doctor who?
How did you guess?

- Who's there?
Orange.
Orange who?
Orange you glad I called?

Will you remember me in one day's time?
Of course I will.
Will you remember me in a week's time?
Of course I will.
Will you remember me in a year's time?
Of course I will.
Will you remember me in ten year's time?
Of course I will.
Knock! Knock!
Who's there?
See—you've forgotten already!

- Who's there?
Madam.
Madam who?
Madam finger's caught in the door.

- Who's there?
Boo.
Boo who?
No need to cry—it's only a joke.

- Who's there?
Olive.
Olive who?
Olive across the road.

- Who's there?
Mommy.
Mommy who?
Mommeasles are better so can I come in?

- Who's there?
Harry.
Harry who?
Harry up and let me in!

- Who's there?
Fanny.
Fanny who?
Fanny the way you keep saying "Who's there?" every time
I knock!

The Birdbrain's Reading List

or bred any good rooks lately?

Parachute Jumping	*by* Willie Maykit
The Inevitable Occurrence	*by* Sue Nora Later
Everybody Out	*by* Rufus Falling
Laying Carpets	*by* Walter Wall
Caring for Parrots	*by* L.O. Polly
Solitude	*by* I. Malone
The Thirsty Diner	*by* Phillipa Carafe
Bricklaying	*by* C. Ment
First in the Class	*by* Hedda De Classe
A Visit to the Dentist	*by* Lord Howard Hertz
Home Haircutting	*by* Shaun Head
End of Term	*by* C. Myra Port
How to Make an Igloo	*by* S. Keemo
Pachyderms	*by* L.E. Fant
Feed Your Dog Properly	*by* Norah Bone
Weight Lifting	*by* Buster Gutt
Spare the Rod and Spoil the Child	*by* Corporal Punishment
Run for Your Lives	*by* General Panic
Designing Placards	*by* Bill Poster
On the Rocks	*by* Mandy Lifeboat

Out on Parole	*by* Freda Convict
Escape to the New Forest	*by* Lucinda Woods
Riding for Plesaure	*by* G.G. Canters
Not Too Fast	*by* Ann Dante

148

Love and Marriage

"I could marry anyone I please."

"So why don't you?"

"I haven't pleased anyone yet."

To everyone's astonishment the middle-aged spinster announced her engagement.

"But I thought you said all men were stupid," said one of her friends, "and that you'd never marry?"

"Yes, I did," she replied, "but then I found one who asked me."

George had reached the age of forty-six, and not only was he still unmarried but he had never even had a girlfriend. "Come along now, George," said his father. "It's high time you got yourself a wife and settled down. Why at your age I'd been married twenty years."

"But that was to Mom," said his son. "You can't expect me to marry a stranger!"

Harry was madly in love with Betty, but couldn't get up enough courage to pop the question face to face. Finally he decided to ask her on the telephone. "Darling!" he blurted out, "will you marry me?"

"Of course, I will, you silly boy," she replied, "who's speaking?"

Poor old Steve sent his photograph off to a Lonely Hearts Club. They sent it back saying they weren't that lonely . . .

"I think my wife is trying to tell me something," said the unfortunate husband, "—she keeps wrapping my sandwiches in a road map!"

Young Andrew was being interviewed by his girlfriend's father. "So," said that august personage, "you want to be my son-in-law, do you?"

"Not particularly," said Andrew tactlessly, "but if I want to marry your daughter I haven't much choice, have I?"

Jim and Mike were in the bar, mulling over Mike's problems. "Alice and I want to get married," said Mike, "but we can't find anywhere to live."

"Why don't you live with Alice's parents?" suggested Jim.

"We can't do that," said Mike, "they're still living with *their* parents!"

Freddie had persuaded Amanda to marry him, and was formally asking her father for his permission. "Sir," he said, "I would like to have your daughter for my wife."

"Why can't she get one of her own?" said Amanda's father, disconcertingly.

"How's your new wife's cooking then, Barry?"

"Not up to much. She can't even boil water without burning it!"

On their first evening in their new home the bride went in to the kitchen to fix drinks. Five minutes later she came back into the living room in tears.

"What's the matter, my angel?" asked her husband anxiously.

"Oh, Derek!" she sobbed, "I put the ice cubes in hot water to wash them and now they've disappeared!"

"After we'd been married two years there was the patter of tiny feet around the house."

"You had a baby?"

"No—mice."

"Why aren't you married?"

"I was born that way."

Mrs. Jones and her little daughter Karen were outside the church watching all the comings and goings of a wedding. After the photographs had been taken, everyone had driven off to the reception, and all the excitement was over, Karen said to her mother, "Why did the bride change her mind, Mommy?"

"How do you mean, change her mind?" asked Mrs. Jones.

"Well," said the moppet, "she went into the church with one man and came out with another!"

"When I grow up," confided little Amy to her uncle, "I'm going to marry the boy next door."

"Why is that?"

"'Cause I'm not allowed to cross the road."

Mr. and Mrs. Harris were celebrating their Silver Anniversary with a big party, at which the center of attraction was a huge cake. "This cake was made by my wife's fair hands," said Mr. Harris proudly. "Every year on our anniversary she makes a cake, and I like to think of them as milestones on our journey through life..."

"Today is my twenty-fifth wedding anniversary."

"Congratulations."

"Yes, I've been married twenty-five times."

"My wife's an angel—she's never got anything to wear, she's always up in the air and forever harping on about something..."

The aged, meek little clerk had asked for an interview with the manager. "Yes, what is it?" demanded the boss aggressively. "I'm very busy."

"I'm so sorry to interrupt you, sir," said the faithful employee, "but I wondered whether it would be possible for me to have tomorrow off."

"Have tomorrow off?!" said the boss. "Good heavens, man, tomorrow is our busiest day of the week! You've had your holidays, why do you want tomorrow off?"

"Well, you see, sir," said the wretched clerk, "tomorrow is my Golden Wedding Anniversary, and my son has arranged a party for my wife and myself, and all our relatives and friends are coming, and—"

"Oh, very well," said the boss with very bad grace, "but don't think I'm going to put up with this every fifty years!"

Two women were talking at a party, and one said, "Look at that awful-looking man over there... isn't he hideous? I think he must be the most unattractive man I've ever seen in my life!"

"That happens to be my husband!" said the second icily.

"Oh dear," said the first, covered in confusion, "I'm so sorry."

To which the unfortunate wife replied, "*You're* sorry...?"

"Do you think, Professor, that my wife should take up the piano as a career?"

"No, I think she should put down the lid as a favor."

"How old is your wife?"

"She's approaching thirty."

"From which direction?"

"I thought you were going to marry Eddie? You said it was love at first sight."

"It was—it was the second and third sights that put me off him."

"It's odd how many girls nowadays don't want to get married," said Bob disconsolately.

"What makes you say that?" asked his friend.

"'Cause I've asked them."

"Why did you refuse to marry Richard, Tessa?"

"'Cause he said he'd die if I didn't and I'm just curious..."

"The man I marry," said the romantic-minded girl, "must be as noble as King Arthur, as brave as Herucles, as wise as Solomon, and as handsome as Apollo!"

"How fortunate we met."

"Why does your husband always call you his Fair Lady when you're a brunet?"

"He's a bus conductor."

"My Peter keeps telling everyone he's going to marry the most beautiful girl in the world."

"What a shame! And after all the time you've been engaged!"

"But she's so young to get married," sobbed Diana's mother. "Only seventeen!"

"Try not to cry about it," said her husband soothingly. "Think of it not as losing a daughter but as gaining a bathroom."

"Will you be my wife one day?"

"Not for one hour, creep."

OFFICE WORKER: "Can I have tomorrow afternoon off, sir? It's my grandmother's funeral."

MANAGER: "Come off it, boy. Didn't you have an afternoon off a couple of months ago because your grandmother died?"

OFFICE WORKER: "Yes, but Grandad married again."

"Your mother has been living with us for six years now," said the long-suffering wife to her husband. "I really think it's time she moved out and found a place of her own."

"*My* mother?" said her bewildered husband, "I thought she was *your* mother!"

"My husband is a man of rare gifts."

"That's nice."

"He hasn't given me a present in twenty-five years of marriage..."

Q: Under law, what is the maximum penalty for bigamy?
A: Two mothers-in-law.

"Last week when I cut my hand badly, my mother-in-law cried over me."

"She's fond of you, is she?"

"No—she just wanted to get salt into the wound."

HUSBAND: Why can't you make bread like my mother?
WIFE: I would if you could make dough like your father!

Grab Bag

"I like your Easter tie."
  "Why do you call it my Easter tie?"
  "It's got egg on it."

I won't say my sister is a bad driver but my Dad's put a glass floor in the car so whenever she runs anyone over she can see who it is.

"Why did you put that spider in my bed?"
  "'Cause I couldn't find a frog."

Can you spell "Blind pig?"
Sure—B.L.I.N.D. P.I.G.
No, it's B.L.N.D.P.G. If it had two eyes it wouldn't be blind!

As the housewife opened her door the salesman opened up his case. "Want any brushes, lady?" he asked.

"No, thank you."

"Dusters?"

"No, thank you."

"Furniture polish? Any cleaning materials at all?"

"No, thank you."

"I thought not," he replied. "The woman next door said you never used any . . . !"

My new neighbor's got a glass eye. Mind you, you'd never know unless it came out in the conversation . . .

My Dad's got a new job. He's a test pilot for Kleenex.

"Last week I took the first step towards getting divorced."

"Did you see a lawyer?"

"No, I got married."

A man whose son had just passed his driving test went home one evening and found that the boy had driven slap into the living room.

"How on earth did you manage to do that?" he fumed.

"Quite simple, Dad. I came in through the kitchen and turned left!"

"Take the wheel, Harry!" said the nervous lady driver. "There's a tree coming straight for us!"

"I hate paying my income tax."

"You should be a good citizen—why don't you pay with a smile?"

"I'd like to but they insist on money . . . !"

"I've just invented a truth drink. One sip and you'll tell the truth."

"May I try some? . . . ugh! That's kerosene!"

"That's the truth!"

"I'd like some bath salts, please, sir."

"Certainly, ma'am. Scented?"

"No, I'll take them with me. And I'd like a mirror."

"Certainly, ma'am. A hand mirror?"

"No, I want to see my face."

"My husband's a wonderful man. I really think he's one in a million."

"Really? I thought he was won in a raffle . . ."

"No, I really don't think I want any insurance," said the homeowner to the salesman.

"Please reconsider, sir. A short time ago one of my clients took out some insurance and the very next day there was a terrible fire at his house—it burned right down! He jumped out of an upstairs window, landed on his car, smashed the roof in and broke both his legs!"

"Yes, well, he was one of the lucky ones."

Did you hear about the Do-It-Yourself funeral? They just loosen the earth and you sink down by yourself.

"Did you know that in Russia they keep a standing army of two million men?"

"They must be very short of chairs in Russia..."

An old lady came across a small boy crying bitterly. "What's the matter, sonny?" she asked.

"Aaaoowww!" he sobbed. "It's my birthday, isn't it? An' I got a bicycle and some roller skates and I'm havin' a party with lots of candy and cake and ice cream an' we're havin' games and a magician—" and again he was overcome with tears.

"That all sounds very nice," said the old lady. "Why are you crying then?"

"'Cause I'm lost, aren't I?!"

The distinguished old man was being interviewed by a journalist. "I understand, sir," said the journalist, "that you have just celebrated your ninetieth birthday?"

"That is correct—ninety years of age and I haven't an enemy in the world."

"That's wonderful, sir."

"Not an enemy in the world. They're all dead!"

"Well, sir, I hope to have the privilege of interviewing you on your one hundredth birthday."

"I don't see why not, young man," said the eminent personage. "You look perfectly fit to me!"

"I got thirty Valentine cards last year."

"Thirty? Wow!"

"But I couldn't afford to post them."

The after-dinner speaker was droning on and on and on, boring everyone to tears. One of the guests, fighting to keep his drooping eyelids open, turned to the lady on his right and said, "Can nothing be done to shut him up?"

"If there is I'd like to know," said the lady, "—I'm his wife and I've been trying to shut him up for twenty years!"

"My grandfather didn't shave till he was thirty years old."

"Where was his beard?"

"Down to his knees!"

Two friends were watching a Clint Eastwood Western film. As Clint rode into town where the bad guys were lying in wait, one said "I bet you $5 he falls off his horse."

"Don't be stupid," said the other, "Clint Eastwood never falls off his horse."

"I bet you he does."

"All right," said the second, "I'll bet you $5 he doesn't!"

They sat in silence watching the film for a few more minutes; the bad guys began shooting, Clint Eastwood's horse reared—and off he fell!

"There! I told you!" said the first viewer.

"Oh, all right," said the second, "here's your $5."

"No, I can't take it," said his friend. "I must confess— I've seen this film before."

"So have I," came the reply, "but I didn't think he'd be such a fool as to fall off again!"

"How old are you?" said one lady to another.

"I'm thirty-nine," was the response. "But I don't look it, do I?"

"No, but you used to..."

The dirty old tramp sidled up to a passerby. "Got a buck for a bed for the night?" he muttered. "No," said the passerby firmly.

"Got fifty cents for a meal?"

"Certainly not."

"Oh... have you got twenty cents for a cup of tea, then?"

"No, I have not."

"Lord—you'd better take my harmonica. You're worse off than I am!"

Later on the same tramp approached a punk rocker. "Here, son—I haven't had a bite for three days," he wheezed. So the punk rocker bit him...

"We had a wonderful act at the club last week—a man who did farmyard impressions."

"What was wonderful about it?"

"He didn't do the sounds—he did the smells..."

A man walked into a theatrical agent's office and asked if he could do an audition. "All right," said the agent, "what sort of an act do you do?"

"I do bird impressions," said the man.

"No, I don't want that," said the agent, "I've got three bird impressionists on my books already."

"Oh, all right," said the man, and flew out of the window.

"Tell me, driver," said the old lady passenger, "does this bus stop at the river?"

"There'll be an awful splash if it doesn't, Ma," said the man.

"Tell me, driver, do you stop at the Ritz Hotel?"

"What—on my salary? You must be joking!"

Mr. Jones met a neighbor carrying a front door. "Why are you carrying that, Tom?" asked Mr. Jones.

"I've lost my key," replied Tom.

"Oh," said Mr. Jones, "so how will you get in?"

"It's all right—I've left the window open."

The moving man was struggling to get a large bureau up the stairs.

"Why don't you get Charlie to help you?" asked the moving foreman, to which the man answered, "Charlie's inside carrying the clothes."

"How long will the next bus be, Officer?"

"About eight yards, sir."

"I'm not at all satisfied with the evidence against you," said the magistrate to the prisoner on trial, "so I shall find you not guilty. You are discharged."

"Oh, good," said the prisoner, "does that mean I can keep the money?"

"I went to my doctor to see if he could help me give up smoking."

"What did he say?"

"He suggested that every time I felt like a smoke I should reach for a bar of chocolate."

"Did that do any good?"

"No—I can't get the chocolate to light."

It so happened that Tony's brother and girlfriend had their birthdays on the same day; for his brother he bought a shotgun and for his girlfriend a bottle of very expensive perfume, for which he wrote a note saying "Use this on yourself and think of me." Unfortunately Tony put the note in with the wrong present...

Three boys called Manners, Shut-up, and Trouble were playing in the woods one day, when Trouble suddenly vanished from sight! Try as they would, Shut-up and Manners were unable to find him; they ran and shouted and ran and shouted, but Trouble had managed to get himself totally lost. So Shut-up and Manners decided to go and report Trouble's disappearance to the police. When they arrived at the police station, Manners waited outside on the steps while Shut-up went in.

"What's your name, sonny?" asked the policeman behind the inquiries desk.

"Shut-up," replied the boy.

"Eh?" said the policeman, startled, "Where's your manners?"

"Sitting outside on the steps," replied Shut-up.

The policeman's brow darkened. "Are you looking for trouble?" he scowled.

"Yes," said Shut-up, "how did you know?"

Three foreigners visiting England went out for a walk to see the sights of London. They could speak very little English—in fact all one could say was "I've just robbed a bank," all the second could say was "Fifty pence," and all the third could say was "Me, too." As they walked along Piccadilly they happened to see a large black dog come hurtling out of a shop and crash into an old lady, knocking her to the pavement. The three foreigners rushed to help her up, and the old lady was suitably grateful for their kind attention and assistance. "Thank you so much," she said, straightening, her hat, "I'm quite all right now."

"I've just robbed a bank," said the first foreigner, smiling.

"Really?" said the old lady in surprise. "How much did you get?"

"Fifty pence," said the second with a grin.

"You naughty person!" scolded the old lady, "you'll go to prison for that!"

To which the third foreigner replied happily, "Me, too!"

Mr. Donovan had spent the evening visiting his old friend Mr. Moore, but when the time came for him to leave there was a sudden thunderstorm and the rain began to fall in torrents.

"You'd better stay the night," said Mr. Moore.

"Thanks, I will," said Mr. Donovan, "I'll just pop home for my pajamas."

Did you hear about the man who went to a Fancy Dress Ball dressed as a biscuit? A dog ate him up in the hall...

"The acoustics in this hall are marvelous, aren't they?"
  "Pardon?"

"I've had to give up tap dancing."
  "Why?"
  "I kept falling in the sink."

"I had a flat tire yesterday."
  "Oh, bad luck. Did you drive over a nail?"
  "No, a milk bottle."
  "A milk bottle? Didn't you see it in the road, then?"
  "No, the silly woman had it hidden under her coat."

The two little boys met while paddling in the sea during their summer vacations.
  "Gosh!" said the first, "your feet are really dirty!"
  "Yes," agreed the second, "we didn't come here last year!"

"Vincent, why have you got a sausage stuck behind your ear?"

"Eh? Oh, gee—I must have eaten my pencil for lunch!"

At a restaurant which prided itself on its wide selection of dishes, a customer was inspecting the menu. "You'll find, sir," said the waiter proudly, "that everything is on the menu. Absolutely everything!"

"Yes, so I see," said the customer tartly, "so take it away and bring me a clean one!"

"Have you got holes in your socks?"

"Certainly not."

"Then how do you get your feet in?"

An Egyptian lady was speaking to a friend on the telephone.

"Come and spend the evening with me," she said, "and if I'm in the bath when you arrive—just Toot 'n' Come In."

Service with a Smile

"Butcher, have you got a sheep's head?"

"No, it's just the way I part my hair."

"Give me a half-pound of bacon, please, and make it lean."

"Certainly, ma'am—which way?"

BARBER: Tell me, sir, when you came in here were you wearing a red scarf?

CUSTOMER: No, I wasn't.

BARBER: Jeez, I've cut your throat!

"Before I can accept a check, ma'am," said the shop cashier, "you will have to identify yourself."

"Very well," said the customer, taking a mirror from her handbag and peering into it. "Yes, it's me."

As the funeral cortege reached the top of the hill the rear door of the hearse came open. To the horror of the mourners the coffin slid out, and then proceeded to bounce and clatter its way right down the hill! At the bottom of the hill its speed carried it right through the open doorway of a drug store where, before the appalled gaze of the druggist, it crashed into the counter causing the lid to spring open. "For goodness' sake," said the corpse, "give me something to stop this coffin . . ."

CUSTOMER: This loaf is lovely and warm!
BAKER: So it should be, ma'am. The cat's been sitting on it all morning!

Did you hear about Paddy who opened a shop next to the Chinese Take-out? He called it an Irish Bring-back . . .

"So you're looking for a job, eh?" said the shopkeeper. "Do you like hard work?"

"No, sir."

"I'll hire you—that's the first honest answer I've had this morning!"

"If I hire you," said the shopkeeper to the youth, "you'll get $60 a week to start with, and $80 in six months."

"I'll come back in six months."

"I'd like some really tight jeans."

"Certainly, sir. Will you walk this way?"

"If they're as tight as yours I'll probably have to."

The old lady walked into a drug store and bought a packet of mothballs. The next day she returned—and again bought a packet of mothballs. On the third day she did the same and when she appeared the fourth day and asked yet again for a packet of mothballs the cashier could not restrain his curiosity. "You must have a lot of moths, ma'am?" he queried.

"Yes, I have," she nodded, "and I don't know what I'm going to do. I've been throwing these balls at them for three days now and I haven't hit one yet!"

A woman rushed into a hardware store and said, "Can I have a mousetrap, please? And will you be quick—I've a bus to catch."

"Sorry, ma'am," said the assistant, "we don't sell 'em that big!"

A man dashed into a cafe and said to the woman behind the counter, "Can you give me a glass of water, please?"

"Here you are, dear," she said, handing it over. But to her astonishment the man ran out of the cafe without drinking it. Two minutes later he was back with the empty glass. "Can I have another glass of water, please?"

"Certainly, dear," she said in kindly fashion. "But why don't you drink it here?"

"Oh, it's not for drinking," he said. "My house is on fire!"

Sports Mad

During a baseball game there was a telephone call in the pavilion for one of the players whose abilities as a batter were considerably below par. "He's not here at the moment," said the coach. "He's just going up to bat."

"Oh, all right," said the caller, "I'll hold on!"

"May I go swimming, Mommy?"

"No, you may not. There are sharks here."

"But Daddy's swimming."

"He's insured."

At Grotsville United's football field they always play the National Anthem before each match. It isn't that they are all that patriotic—they just like to make sure the team can stand up...

Did you hear about the boxing referee who used to work at a space rocket launching site? If a fighter was knocked down he'd count "Ten, nine, eight, seven..."

"My brother's a professional boxer."

"Heavyweight?"

"No, featherweight. He tickles his opponents to death."

"My brother's a professional boxer."

"Really? What's his name?"

"Rembrandt!"

"Rembrandt?"

"Yes, he's always on the canvas ... you know, he'd have won his last fight only the referee was standing on his hand."

"Sorry I missed that field goal, skipper," said the useless forward. "I could kick myself, I really could."

"Don't bother—you'd only miss."

"My dog plays chess."

"Your dog plays chess? He must be very clever!"

"Oh, I don't know. I usually beat him three times out of four."

"Out!" said the umpire.

"Out?" yelled the outraged batter, "what for?"

"For the rest of the afternoon."

As any serious angler knows the best time to fish is at night, so two friends agreed to meet in the town bar and then to go fishing at closing time. Unfortunately they drank too much beer, and closing time saw them staggering out with their rods and their reels, very much the worse for wear. But they managed to reach a bridge without mishap, baited their lines, cast into the darkness and sat down to wait for a bite. But their luck was out, hour after hour they sat with their lines remaining motionless, listening to the clock in the town church distantly chiming the night away. By the time dawn was just about to break they were cold, tired, fed up and sober, and had just decided to pack it in and go home—when the 6:30 express train to Boston pulled their rods out of their hands...

"I say, look here!" said an angry member of the grouse-shooting party. "You nearly shot my wife!"

"I'm terribly sorry," said the short-sighted offender, "shall I try again?"

"I say, look here!" said another even angrier member of the party. "You just shot my wife!"

"Oh, have I?" said the same offender. "Here—have a crack at mine!"

The big-game hunter was showing his friends his hunting trophies. Drawing their attention to a lion-skin rug on the floor he said, "I shot this fellow in Africa. Didn't want to kill such a magnificent beast, of course, but it was either him or me."

"Well," said a guest, "he certainly makes a better rug than you would!"

Having just swam the Channel, the exhausted swimmer staggered up the beach at Calais. *"Formidable!"* enthused a Frenchman. "You 'ave performed the great foot!"

"It's feat, actually," said the English swimmer.

The Frenchman's eyebrows lifted in astonishment. "So you 'ave swum both ways—*incroyable!*"

"I'm awarding a free kick," said the football referee firmly.

"Who to?" asked a bewildered player.

"Us," said the referee.

A distraught golfer rushed into the club house and yelled to the steward "Quick, ring for an ambulance! I think I've killed my wife! She was standing closer to me than I thought and when I swung back to hit the ball I clouted her on the head. She dropped like a stone and I can't rouse her!"

"Which club were you using?" asked the steward calmly.

"Which club?" asked the panic-stricken husband, "Er— a number five iron, I think."

"Yes," nodded the steward. "That's the club."

"Did you go water-skiing on vacation?"

"No. I couldn't find a lake with a slope."

"Hey, you!" yelled the ranger to the small boy. "Can't you read that sign? No fishing in this river."

"I'm not fishing," came the perky reply. "I'm just teaching my worm how to swim!"

"How should I have played that last shot?" the bad golfer asked his partner.

"Under an assumed name."

Why should a golfer aways wear two pairs of trousers?

In case he gets a hole in one.

A layman and a vicar were playing golf one day, and the layman was not having a good game. "Oh, darn, I missed!" he said at the first green, missing an easy putt. "Oh, darn, I missed again!" he said at the second green as he missed another easy putt. And so it went on—every time he played a bad shot, he would say, "Oh, darn, I missed!"

The vicar put up with this for half the round, but then felt he owed it to the dignity of his calling to remonstrate with the layman. "You really must not keep using such dreadful language, my dear sir,' he said, "or the Lord may well strike you down!"

And just as the words were out of his mouth there came a jagged flash of lightning—and in a split second the vicar was burnt to a crisp! Above the rolling thunderclouds a deep voice was heard to say, "Oh, darn, I've missed!"

Why was Cinderella kicked out of the soccer team?
'Cause she kept running away from the ball.

"The manager of the Cosmos said I'd be a great soccer player if it weren't for two things."
"What were they?"
"My feet."

"Every night of my life I dream about baseball. Always I'm playing an eternal game of baseball. Do you think there's something wrong with me?"
"Don't you ever dream about girls?"
"What? And miss my innings?!"

"I went fly-fishing yesterday."
"Catch anything?"
"Yes. A 3 pound bluebottle."

An avid golfer was talking to his vicar one Sunday after morning service. "Tell me, vicar," said the sportsman, "do you suppose there is a golf course in Heaven? I should very much like to think so."

"I'm really not sure," said the clergyman. "I've never thought about it before. I'll tell you what—the next time I talk to God I'll ask Him."

The following Sunday again saw the avid golfer talking to the vicar after morning service. "Well?" he asked. "did you get any answer?"

"Yeees," said the vicar slowly, "I have good news and bad news. The good news is that there *is* a golf course in Heaven."

"And the bad news?"

"You are booked in for a round tomorrow afternoon!"

Hey Diddle Riddle!

What did the envelope say to the stamp?
  "Stick with me, baby, and we'll go places!"

Why is tennis a noisy game?
  'Cause when you play it you have to raise a racket.

What is a happy tin in the United States?
  A-merry-can.

Why did the nurse creep into the cupboard?
  So as not to wake the sleeping pills.

What room has no walls, floor, ceiling, or windows?
  A mushroom.

What is the invention that enables you to see through the thickest walls?
  A window.

Why did the man throw his watch out of the window?
  To see time fly.

What runs but has no legs?
  A tap.

What has a neck but no head?
  A bottle.

Why is a rabbit's nose always shiny?
  'Cause it keeps its powder puff at the wrong end.

Why couldn't the leopard escape from the zoo?
  'Cause he was always spotted.

If there are two tomatoes on a plate, which is the cowboy?
  Neither—they're both redskins.

What is the fastest vegetable in the world?
  A scarlet runner bean.

Why is the letter A like a flower?
  'Cause the B comes after it.

Why did the rooster cross the road?
  For his own fowl purposes.

What nut has no shell?
  A doughnut.

What walks on its head all day?
  A thumbtack stuck in your shoe.

What did the jack say to the car?
  "Can I give you a lift?"

Why do we sing Hymns in church and not Hers?
  Because they all finish with Amen and not Awomen.

What trees do fingers and thumbs grow on?
    Palm trees.

What is worse than a giraffe with a sore neck?
    A centipede with corns.

If pigskin made good shoes, what can you make with banana skin?
    Slippers.

What has a bottom at the top?
    A leg.

What did one eye say to the other eye?
    Something's come between us that smells.

Why did the soccer manager give his team a lighter?
    'Cause they kept losing their matches.

What has a bed but does not sleep? What has a mouth but does not speak?
    A river.

Why was the little boy glad that everyone called him Cyril?
  'Cause that was his name.

Name a shooting star.
  Clint Eastwood.

Can a shoe box?
  No, but a tin can.

Have you ever seen a salad bowl?
  No, but I've seen a square dance.

What coat do you put on only when it's wet?
  A coat of paint.

What is the similarity between soldiers and dentists?
  They both have to drill.

When should you feed tiger's milk to a baby?
  When it's a baby tiger.

What tongue never speaks?
    The tongue in your shoe.

What is a calf after it is one year old?
    A two-year-old calf.

Why is a river rich?
    Because it has two banks.

What did one rose say to the other rose?
    Hiya, Bud.

Why is a baby like an old car?
    Because both have a rattle.

What does the sea say to the sand?
    Nothing—it waves.

What letters are not in the alphabet?
    Those that are in the mailbox.

What is the hardest thing about learning to ride a bike?
  The pavement.

What colors should you paint the sun and the wind?
  The sun rose and the wind blew.

If your clock strikes thirteen, what time is it?
  Time to get a new clock.

Why did the man comb his hair with his toes?
  To make ends meet.

What is the definition of a harp?
  A nude piano.

What does a deaf fisherman need?
  A herring aid.

What are crispy, round, greasy, and romantic?
  Chips that pass in the night.

How can you jump off a fifty-foot ladder in complete safety?
    You jump off the bottom rung.

If two is company and three is a crowd, what's four and five?
    Nine.

Why did the old retiree put wheels on his rocking chair?
    'Cause he wanted to rock 'n' roll.

What do cannibals have for lunch?
    Baked beings.

What did the pig say when the chef cut off his tail?
    "This is the end of me..."

Why was the cowboy always in trouble?
    'Cause he couldn't stop horsing around.

What must you know to be an auctioneer?
    Lots.

Why did the teenager not want to work in the fabric firm?
   'Cause she was too young to dye.

Who were the first gamblers?
   Adam and Eve, 'cause they had a pair o' dice (Paradise).

What happened when the ax fell on the car?
   There was an ax-i-dent.

Why was the crab arrested?
   'Cause he was always pinching things.

When does a horse have six legs?
   When it's got a rider on its back.

Why does a horse have six legs?
   'Cause it has forelegs in front and two behind.

How do you keep an idiot waiting?
   I'll tell you later...

Why should you never gossip in fields?
    'Cause corn has ears, potatoes have eyes, and beanstalk.

What is cowhide most used for?
    Holding cows together.

What has one hundred limbs but cannot walk?
    A tree.

What do we do with trees after we chop them down?
    Chop them up.

What tools do we use in arithmetic?
    Multipliers.

What water won't freeze?
    Boiling water.

What occurs once in every minute, twice in every moment, but not once in a thousand years?
    The letter M.

What wears a coat all winter and pants in the summer?
  A dog.

What's shut when it's open and open when it's shut?
  A drawbridge.

What training do you need to be a garbage collector?
  None, you pick it up as you go along.

What gets wetter as it dries?
  A towel.

When is a black dog not a black dog?
  When it's a greyhound.

Why did Kojak throw away the keys?
  'Cause he didn't have any locks.

What would you call five bottles of lemon soda?
  A pop group.

What do you take off last when you get into bed?
  Your feet off the floor.

What should you do for a starving cannibal?
  Give him a hand.

What did one tomato say to the other?
  "You go on ahead and I'll ketchup."

What is it that men do standing up, ladies do sitting down, and dogs on three legs?
  Shake hands.

What happens if pigs fly?
  Bacon goes up.

What did the crook get who stole the calendar?
  Twelve months.

If an apple a day keeps the doctor away, what does a clove of garlic do?
  Keeps *everyone* away!

What does the winner of a track meet always lose?
　His breath.

Why are Frenchmen cannibals?
　'Cause they like eating Frogs' legs.

Why was Christopher Columbus a crook?
　'Cause he double-crossed the Atlantic.

What nut sounds like a sneeze?
　A cashew!

What did the pilot say as he left the bar?
　Must fly now!

Why are cooks cruel?
　'Cause they beat eggs and batter fish.

Why do white sheep eat more grass than black sheep?
　'Cause there are more of them.

What happened to the man who listened to a match?
　　He burned his ear.

Why is there no tug-of-war match between England and France?
　　'Cause no one can find a rope twenty-six miles long!

Why did the orange stop rolling?
　　'Cause it ran out of juice.

NEWS FLASH:
　　1,000 MATTRESSES STOLEN. POLICE ARE SPRINGING INTO ACTION!

HOLE FOUND IN WALL OF NUDIST COLONY. POLICE ARE LOOKING INTO IT!

What did Paul Revere say at the end of his midnight ride?
　　Whoooaaaa!

Who has the biggest boots in the British Army?
　　The soldier with the biggest feet.

What gets bigger the more you take out?
   A hole.

What happened to the man who couldn't tell porridge from putty?
   All his windows fell out.

Why will the world never end?
   'Cause it's round.

Why doesn't the sea ever fall into space?
   It's tide.

What is a waste of energy?
   Telling a hair-raising story to a bald man!

What did Mrs. Spider say when Mr. Spider broke her new web?
   Darn it!

Waiter Minute!

Hey, waiter! There are some coins in my soup!
Well, you said you wanted some change in
your meals.

- I've only got one piece of meat!
  All right, I'll cut it in two for you.

- What about meat balls?
  I've never been to any.

- There's a button in my lettuce!
  That must be from the salad dressing.

- This egg's bad!
  Don't blame me. I only lay the table.

- How long will my pizza be?
  We don't do long ones, sir. Only round.

- What's this fly doing in my soup?
  Looks like the backstroke, sir.

- I've just found a maggot in my salad!
  That's better than finding half a maggot,
  isn't it?

- There's a fly in my soup!
  You'll have to get it out yourself. I can't
  swim.

- What's this fly doing in my wine?
  You did ask for something with body in
  it.

- Why is my food all mushed up?
  You did ask me to step on it, sir.

- You've brought me the wrong order!
  Well, you did say you wanted something
  different.

- This soup is terrible! Call the manager!
  He won't eat it either, sir.

- Bring me a dragon sandwich.
  Sorry, sir. We've run out of bread.

- What's this fly doing in my soup?
  Looks like he's trying to get out, sir.

- There's a cockroach in my soup!
  That's strange—it's usually a fly.

- There's a frog in my soup!
  Yes, sir. The fly's on holiday.

- There's a fly in my soup.
  That's all right, sir. There's a spider on
  your roll.

- Bring me a crocodile sandwich immediately.
  I'll make it snappy, sir.

- What do you charge for dinner?
  $10 a head, sir.
  Very well. Just bring me an ear.

- What's in this Hungarian Goulash?
  Only genuine Hungarians, sir.

- What's wrong with this fish?
  Long time, no sea.

- There's a fly playing around in my saucer!
  Yes, sir. Next week he hopes to be playing in the cup.

- This plate's dirty.
  The thumb mark's mine but the egg-stain's from yesterday.

- There's a fly in my alphabet soup!
  I expect he's learning to read.

- There's a fly in my soup!
  The little rascals don't care what they eat, do they?

- There's a fly in my soup!
  Yes, the chef used to be a tailor.

- There's a fly in my soup!
  That's not a fly—it's the last customer. The chef's a witch doctor.

- Waiter, would you say you were an independent-minded person?
  I would indeed, sir. I don't take orders from anyone.

- Do you play tennis?
  Oh, yes. I really know how to serve.

There's a fly in my soup!
Don't worry, sir, he won't drink much.

- There's a spider in my soup!
Oh, really? That's 10 cents extra.

Comic Situations

BOSS: "What's your name?"
NEW BOY: "Herbert Harris."
BOSS: "Say 'sir' when you address me."
NEW BOY: "All right. Sir Herbert Harris."

Did you hear about the really high-powered business tycoon? He had a tall secretary for taking dictation in longhand, a small secretary for taking dictation in shorthand, and a tiny secretary for taking footnotes!

"Don't you like being a telegraph linesman?"
    "No, it's driving me up the pole."

"Your reference is excellent. Apparently your last employer considered you a real live-wire salesman. What were you selling?"
    "Live wires."

"I thought, Jessop, that you wanted yesterday afternoon off because you were seeing your dentist?"

"That's right, sir."

"So how come I saw you coming out of Yankee Stadium at the end of the game with a friend?"

"That was my dentist."

"Why did you leave your last job, Miss Lovejoy?"

"The boss kept kissing me."

"Oh, indeed? Then I can understand why you wanted to quit."

"Yes. I can't stand beards."

"There's only one honest way to make money."

"What's that?"

"I thought you wouldn't know it!"

The apprentice electrician was on his first job. "Take hold of those two wires, Alec," said his master, "and rub them together." Alec did as he was bid, and his master said, "D'you feel anything?"

"No," said Alec.

"That's good—so don't touch those other two wires or you'll get a nasty shock!"

Sally had applied for a bookkeeping job, and was being tested on her ability with figures. "Tell me," said the manager, "if you were to buy something for $8.73 and sell it for $9.42, would you make a profit or a loss?"

Sally screwed up her forehead in concentration, doodled

on her notepad, and then said, "Well, I'd make a profit on the dollars and a loss on the cents."

The young lad had applied for a job, and was asked his full name.

"Aloysius Montmorency Geoghan," he replied.

"How do you spell that?" asked the manager.

"Er—sir—er—can't you just put it down without spelling it?"

"Did your previous employer give you a reference?"

"Yes, but I left it at home."

"What does it say?"

"Er, well, it says I was one of the best employees he had ever fired..."

"Miss Gimlet," said the shop manager, "you really must be more polite to our customers. This morning old Mrs. Scatter came to me with a very serious complaint."

"Why?" asked Miss Gimlet pertly, "are you a doctor?"

"If you're going to work here, young man," said the boss, "one thing you must learn is that we are very keen on cleanliness in this firm. Did you wipe your feet on the mat as you came in?"

"Oh, yessir."

"And another thing we are very keen on is truthfulness: there is no mat."

"How's that new boy getting on, Jarman?" asked the squire.

"I've found something suited to him at last, squire," said the head gardener.

"Good. What's that?"

"Chasing snails off the paths!"

The work manager discovered four of his men hidden in a corner of the warehouse playing cards. "Come along now, men, come along!" he said shortly. "Haven't you anything else to do?"

"Oh yes, sir," said one of the slackers. "There's always darts."

"Why did you leave your last employment?"

"The boss accused me of stealing a five dollar bill."

"But why didn't you make him prove it?"

"He did."

"Miss Cosgrove," said the boss to his secretary, "I have to reply to someone whose christian name is Shirley. Do you think that is a man or a woman?"

"It could be either, sir."

"Yes . . . how can I start the letter then? I can't put Dear Sir or Dear Madam if I don't know, can I?"

"How about starting it, 'Dear Shir . . . ?!'"

"What did his lordship say when you smashed up his Rolls-Royce?"

"Don't know. I never caught his last words."

The flighty young girl was being interviewed for a job.

"You are not married, are you?" asked the boss.

"No, but I've had several near Mrs."

CHIEF CLERK: "Miss Robbins, who put those hideous flowers on my desk?"

SECRETARY: "I did, Mr. Rumball."

CHIEF CLERK: "And who told you to do that?"

SECRETARY: "The manager's wife, Mr. Rumball."

CHIEF CLERK: "Don't they look nice?"

The manager of a shop observed one of his customers in a furious argument with a junior assistant. As he hurried over the customer finally yelled, ". . . and I shall never come into this place again!" And he stalked out, slamming the door behind him. "Hicks," said the shop manager severely, "how many more times must I tell you: the customer is always right!"

"As you wish, sir," said the junior. "He was saying you were a lop-eared, bald-headed, brainless twit!"

"Sir, there's a debt collector in the outer office."

"Tell him he can take that pile on my desk."

A bricklayer was continually being harried by his foreman to work faster. "Let up on us a bit, sir," the worker finally protested. "Rome wasn't built in a day, you know."

"Maybe not," said the foreman, "but I wasn't on that site."

"I need a smart boy," said the boss to the young applicant. "Someone quick to take notice."

"Oh, I can do that, sir. I had it twice last week!"

"I've come in answer to your ad for a handyman."

"And are you handy?"

"Couldn't be handier. I live next door."

WORKER: "I bet the boss was furious when you told him I'd be leaving next week."

FOREMAN: "Yes, he was. He thought it was this week."

"Here you are, Davidson," said the boss to a notoriously lazy employee. "Here's your pay for forty hours' slacking!"

"Be fair, man," said the indolent one. "Forty-*one* hours!"

"Why did you leave your last job?"

"Something the boss said."

"Was he abusive?"

"Not exactly."

"What did he say, then?"

"You're fired!"

"You play fair with me and I'll play fair with you," said the boss to the new worker. "Just remember: you can't do too much for a good employer."

"Don't worry, I won't."

"I just want you to remember one thing, Boyce," said the managing director to the new sales manager. "If at first you don't succeed—you're fired!"

"Come on, slowpoke," said the foreman to a lazy worker. "The morning's disappeared."

"Well, don't look at me, man. I didn't take it!"

There had been an explosion in the gunpowder factory, and the management was holding an inquiry into the cause of the accident. "Now, Parsley," said the chairman of the board, "You were on the spot. Exactly what happened?"

"It was like this, sir," explained Parsley, "Old Charlie Higgins was in the mixing room, and I saw him—absent-minded, like—take out a box of matches to have a smoke."

"He struck a match in the mixing room?" said the chairman in horror. "How long had Higgins worked for us?"

"About twenty years, sir."

"Twenty years, and he struck a match in the mixing room? I'd have thought that would be the last thing he'd do."

"It was, sir."

"You're asking a lot of money for an unskilled man," said the foreman to a job applicant, "and you've no experience of our kind of work at all, have you?"

"No, well," explained the hopeful one, "I think I ought to get more money 'cause it's so much harder when you don't know nothing about it, ain't it?"

The butcher's boy had been dismissed for insolence, and vowed vengeance on his ex-employer. The following Saturday morning, when the shop was packed with people buying their weekend roasts, he marched in, elbowed his way to the counter and slapped down one very, very dead cat. "There you are, sir!" he called out cheerily, "that makes up the dozen you ordered!"

"I've worked here for three years now, sir, and during most of that time I've been doing the work of three men. So what about a raise in salary?"

"I can't see my way to giving you a raise, Phillips," said the skinflint boss, "but I'll tell you what I'll do. I'll sack the other two men!"

MASTER CARPENTER: "Son, you're certainly hammering those nails in like lightning!"
APPRENTICE: "You mean I'm fast?"
MASTER CARPENTER: "No—you never strike in the same place twice!"

"I was a waiter at the Hotel Splendiferous for three months, but I had to leave on account of the head waiter's nerves."
"His nerves?"
"He couldn't stand the sound of breaking china."

"Witherspoon, I gave you half a day off because you said you had to tend your prize garden, and now I have been informed that you do not have a garden. What have you to say for yourself?"

"Well, sir, if you've been told there is no garden someone must have pushed it off the window ledge!"

An apprentice blacksmith was told by his master to make a hammer. The lad had not the slightest idea how to begin, so he thought he'd be crafty and slip out and buy one. He duly showed the new hammer to his master who said, "That's excellent boy! Now make fifty more just like it!"

"The first thing you can do," said the boss to the new office boy, "is to look up a telephone number for me. I want to call Mr. Henry T. Zachary—got it?"

"Henry T. Zachary, sir," said the lad, reaching for the directory. "Right away, sir."

Half an hour later the manager called the boy into his office. "Come in," he said, "how are you doing with that number?"

"It's coming along, sir," replied the eager youngster. "I'm up to the M's already!"

The beautiful film star was giving her chauffeur/handyman a severe scolding. "Harry," she said firmly, "I must ask you not to come into my bathroom or my bedroom without knocking. Is that quite clear?"

"Don't worry, miss," responded the aggrieved servant, "I always looks through the key hole first, an' if you got nothing on I don't come in!"

"How many people work in this office?"

"About half of them, sir."

The pert young typist arrived at the office late as usual. "Mary!" called the supervisor, "don't you know what time we start work here?"

"No," said the saucy miss, "you're always at it by the time I arrive!"

"May I have an hour off to get my hair cut, sir?"

"Certainly not. Have it cut on your own time."

"But it grows in office hours, sir."

"It doesn't do all it's growing during office hours, boy."

"I'm not cutting it all off!"

The chief clerk answered the telephone, and an aged quavery voice said, "Oh, excuse me, but would it be possible to speak to Darren, the messenger boy?"

"Who is it speaking?" asked the chief clerk.

"This is his grandfather."

"I'm afraid Darren isn't here. He's gone to your funeral!"

"Why do you want next Wednesday off, Carstairs?"

"I'm getting married, sir."

"Getting married?! Great Scott, what feeble-minded girl would want to marry you?"

"Your daughter, sir."

"Mossop! Why are you late this morning?"

"I got married, sir."

"Very well, but see that it doesn't happen again."

"Brendan," scolded his mother, "you've been at that job five years and you're still the office junior. When are you going to get ahead?"

"I've already got one, Mom."

"Rachel, this tea you've made tastes like dishwater!"

"Does it, sir? How can you tell . . . ?"

"Very well, my boy," said the manager, "I'll take you on. I take it you're not afraid of early hours?"

"Oh, no, sir," said the teenage applicant, "you can't close too early for me!"

"Doreen!" said the boss crossly, "I can never find what I want in these files. What system do you use?"

"The Biblical system, sir."

"The Biblical system? What's that?"

"'Seek and ye shall find'!"

The new and very miserable elevator boy on his first morning at work failed to recognize the managing director. "Don't you know who I am, boy?" roared the offended boss.

"No," sniveled the wretched youth.

"You don't? How long have you been here?"

"All damn mornin' . . . !"

That afternoon the elevator boy was required to take the managing director from the twentieth floor to the ground floor. In the lad's inexpert hands the lift roared down the shaft and came to a shuddering, clattering halt at the bottom. "Er—was that stop too quick, sir?" he asked nervously.

"No, not at all," said the managing director heavily. "I always wear my trousers around my ankles!"

"So you want a job with us, do you?" the boss asked the boy. "What's your name?"

"Roy Rogers, sir."

"Roy Rogers, eh?" said the manager jocularly. "Well, that's a well-known name, isn't it?"

"It should be," said the lad proudly. "I've been delivering papers around here for years!"

"Have you any experience with machines?" the foreman asked the youth.

"Yeah—slot and pinball!"

"You're late for work again, Lamport!"

"Yes, I'm sorry, sir. I overslept."

"I thought I told you to get an alarm clock?"

"I did, sir, but there are nine of us in our family."

"What's that got to do with it?"

"The alarm was only set for eight!"

Yuletide Yaks

Harry was always very sentimental about Christmas. Every year he'd take his socks off and stand them up by the fireplace.

Why does Santa Claus come down chimneys?
  Because they soot him.

"We had my Granny for Christmas dinner last year."
  "Really? We had turkey."

"I tell you what I like about Christmas. Kissing girls under the mistletoe."
  "I prefer kissing them under the nose."

One unfortunate girl was so ugly that at Christmas time the boys used to hang her up and kiss the mistletoe...

"I bought my wife a wonderful present for Christmas—a mink outfit."

"Really?"

"Two steel traps and a gun."

George was born on 24 December. He said he wanted to be home in time for Christmas.

Little Susie had made a creche for Christmas, with the shepherds and the animals and the Holy Family, and her handiwork was being admired by a fond aunt. "But what's that thing in the corner?" asked Aunt Gladys.

"Oh, that's the TV," replied Susie proudly.

Only a week after Christmas an irate Mom stormed into the toy stop. "I'm bringing back this unbreakable toy fire-engine," she said to the man behind the counter. "It's useless!"

"Surely your son hasn't broken it already?" he asked.

"No, he's broken all his *other* toys with it!"

Central heating has ruined Christmas—how can Santa Claus slide down radiators?

Who is the meanest man in the world? The father who goes out of the house on Christmas Eve, fires a gun, comes back in and says to his children:

"No presents this Christmas—Santa Claus just shot himself!"

213

Old Granny Harbottle was a very stubborn and independent-minded lady. It didn't matter how cold it was she would insist on getting the coal in her nightie! Even in the depths of winter there she'd be—down the garden, in the shed, getting the coal in her nightie!! One Christmas the neighbors all got together to buy her a shovel but she said her nightie held more...

"I never had a sled when I was a kid. We were too poor."
"What a shame! What did you do when it snowed?"
"Slid down the hills on my cousin."

"For our next Christmas dinner I'm going to cross a chicken with an octopus."
"What on earth for?"
"So we can all have a leg each."

"Here's your Christmas present. A box of your favorite chocolates."
"Ooo, thanks! But it's half empty!"
"Well, they're my favorite chocolates, too..."

Verse and Worse

There was a young lady called Hardwick,
By a baseball she was struck.
And now you can read on her tombstone:
"Hardwick, hard ball, hard luck"!

Hickory Dickory Dock,
Three mice ran up the clock.
The clock struck one,
And the other two got away with minor injuries.

July the Fourth has come and gone,
But thoughts of it still linger.
I held a firecracker in my hand—
Has anybody seen my finger?

The Dachshund's a dog of German descent;
Whose tail never knew where his front end went.

Mary had a little lamb,
It leapt around the hops.
It gamboled in the road one day,
And finished up as chops.

Mary Rose
Sat on a pin.
Mary Rose.

'Twas in a cafe that they first met,
Romeo and Juliet.
And there he first ran into debt—
Ro-me-owed for what Juli-ate!

A famous painter
Met his death;
Because he couldn't
Draw his breath.